Strategic Planning for Small Business Made Easy

Additional titles in Entrepreneur's Made Easy Series

- ▶ *Business Plans Made Easy: It's Not As Hard As You Think* by Mark Henricks
- ▶ *Advertising Without an Agency Made Easy* by Kathy Kobliski
- ▶ *Meetings Made Easy: The Ultimate Fix-It Guide* by Frances Micale
- ▶ *Accounting and Finance for Small Business Made Easy: Secrets You Wish Your CPA Had Told You* by Robert Low

Entrepreneur® MADE EASY *Series*

STRATEGIC PLANNING FOR SMALL BUSINESS MADE EASY

FRED L. FRY
CHARLES R. STONER
LAURENCE G. WEINZIMMER

EP
Entrepreneur®
Press

Editorial Director: Jere Calmes
Cover Design: Beth Hansen-Winter
Editorial and Production Services: CWL Publishing Enterprises, Inc., Madison,
Wisconsin, www.cwlpub.com

This publication is designed to provide accurate and authoritative information in
regard to the subject matter covered. It is sold with the understanding that the
publisher is not engaged in rendering legal, accounting, or other professional services. If legal advice or other expert assistance is required, the services of a competent professional person should be sought.
—From a Declaration of Principles jointly adopted by
a Committee of the American Bar Association and
a Committee of Publishers and Associations

ISBN 1-932531-36-X

Printed in Canada

10 09 08 07 06 05   10 9 8 7 6 5 4 3 2 1

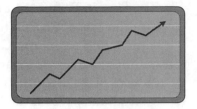

Contents

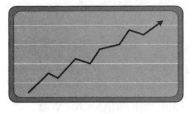

Preface

THIS BOOK IS ABOUT STRATEGIES AND GROWTH—HOW TO CREATE A plan for growth and how to actually make it happen. In the following pages, we provide an easy-to-follow process that can lead to phenomenal results.

We realize that building strategies to grow your business may be one of the most exciting opportunities you will face in your professional career. Yet, we also know that strategic planning can be one of the greatest challenges you will encounter. Let's face it: there is a lot on the line when you try to grow your business. While the potential to grow your business is real, uncertainty and risk cloud the horizon. It is not surprising that few of the millions of business operating today will successfully achieve growth.

We are convinced that the ideas contained in *Strategic Planning Made Easy* can help you achieve the growth you desire. Why? Stated simply, careful strategic thinking and well-designed strategic planning make a difference. Leading companies, regardless of their industries, believe in and adhere to the ideas that we present in this book.

You will find *Strategic Planning Made Easy* to be meaningful, practical, and engaging reading. Straightforward advice and guides will lead you through the process of creating a winning plan for growth. We reinforce our guidelines with numerous examples that illustrate how other companies have used these tools to successfully grow their businesses. You'll recognize some high-profile success stories. Additionally, unlike other planning books, we also include examples of companies that may be much like yours—those on the brink of taking that next step. The ideas presented have been subjected to the "tests of fire." Time and time again, these principles have been used by successful business leaders as they have successfully traveled their journeys of growth.

Overall, we think you will find *Strategic Planning Made Easy* to be a valuable companion for you as build a growing business. Good luck!

Acknowledgments

We are grateful to a number of people who have encouraged and supported this effort. Thanks to our colleagues throughout the country. Your suggestions have helped frame the contents of this book, as well as three earlier strategic planning books. Rather than attempting to name every person (and thereby assuredly making unfortunate omissions), we would simply like to thank our academic and business assistance colleagues for their insights. You have helped this book be grounded in solid strategic thinking.

To all the business managers and leaders who have shown confidence in us and allowed us to "practice" our planning ideas in their organizations, we offer our gratitude. You have allowed this book to be grounded in experience.

Sandra Perry, our department chair, and Robert Baer, dean of the Foster College of Business at Bradley University must be thanked. They have upheld a climate of support that encourages our efforts, as it has over the years. They have helped make this book an extension of our professional commitment.

We offer a special thanks to Jere Calmes, Editorial Director of Entrepreneur Press. Jere not only suggested the concept for this book to us, but he made it happen.

Finally, our thanks to our spouses—Lois, Julie, and Beth. Once again, their support and encouragement has allowed us to do what we enjoy doing.

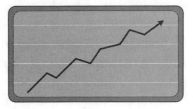

Chapter 1

From Ordinary to Extraordinary

IT IS A CLASSIC STORY—A RECIPE FOR SUCCESS. MIX AN ENTERPRISING ENTREpreneur with a solid business concept, and the sky is the limit.

It's been a fascinating trip for John Schnatter. In 1984, he started his business by working out of a converted broom closet in the back of Mick's Lounge, a tavern owned by his father. His initial $1,600 investment in equipment was funded by selling his cherished Z28 Camaro. His first customers were Mick's patrons, who raved about the pizza John offered. Seeing the opportunity, John didn't hesitate. In 1985, he opened his first restaurant. His guiding business philosophy was simple—"focus on one thing and try to do it better than anyone else." That focus on a streamlined menu and a commitment to quality has not changed. But the scope of John Schnatter's business certainly has. Today, with over 2,800 restaurants in 49 states and 16 international markets, Papa John's Pizza is a favorite. Papa John's has been rated the top pizza brand in the country and John Schnatter has been honored as the Entrepreneur of the Year.[1]

John Schnatter's story is unique, but the pattern is not. It parallels the stories of other well-known legends—Sam Walton, Bill Gates, and Michael Dell. The businesses started by Schnatter, Walton, Gates, and Dell are extraordinary. They are different from ordinary businesses. Of course, there are many reasons for the differences—good ideas, great timing, well-gauged risk taking, and hard work. There is one more essential—an understanding of and commitment to growth and strategic thinking!

Let's look at the differences between ordinary and extraordinary. You will see that Schnatter, Walton, Gates, and Dell compete with ordinary businesses in ordinary industries—pizzas, retail, and computer software and hardware. But the founders of these businesses built something that was clearly out of the ordinary. They were extraordinary.

The Ordinary

Consider ordinary businesses first. There is nothing wrong with ordinary businesses. There are some 25 million of them in the U.S. at any given time. Their founders, owners, and managers are intelligent people who make good business decisions day after day. They meet a payroll, they watch expenses, they get financing, they do some marketing, and many of them report a nice profit at the end of the year. Most are privately held; some are public companies. The vast majority are small, but many ordinary businesses are quite large, employing thousands of workers. And interestingly, the owners of most ordinary businesses are happy with their results. Although we would all like to be rich, owners of many ordinary businesses are really quite happy with their situation in life.

The key to ordinary businesses is this: the owners think like ordinary businesspeople.

What makes an ordinary business ordinary? What makes it start small and stay small or perhaps grow very slowly over decades? What makes a large company become stagnant? The owners are not stupid. They may not even be complacent. But the key to ordinary businesses is this: the owners think like ordinary businesspeople. They make decisions like ordinary businesspeople. They even plan like ordinary businesspeople. But they are not extraordinary!

The Extraordinary: What Makes Businesses Successful

Now consider the Michael Dells of the business world, or the John Schnatters, or the Sam Waltons. Or perhaps consider Richard Schulze. Schulze was a classic entrepreneur. He started with a single music store business that grew into nearly 2,000 stores. Though you may not have heard of Richard Schulze, you have undoubtedly heard of his business: Best Buy. Best Buy is still one of the fastest-growing businesses. In 2004, it had over 750 retail stores encompassing nearly 30 million square feet. It is, indeed, large now. The more important fact, however, is that in fiscal 2004 its sales grew 17 percent!

So what is different about extraordinary leaders and the businesses they have founded? What do they do differently? How do they think differently?

Indeed, thinking differently is what separates the extraordinary from the ordinary. The difference is their intense focus on growth and the planning necessary to achieve it. Along with that, they have an uncanny knack for looking at their market—their customers. They know how customers think and how they buy. And they use their skills to capture the market!

Don't focus solely on a few charismatic leaders such as Schnatter or Walton or Schulze. There are several thousand businesses that fit our definition of extraordinary. These are businesses that grow at perhaps double or triple the rate of other businesses in the same industry. These businesses have moved from ordinary to extraordinary.

So, how do they do it? How do seemingly ordinary businesses transform themselves into extraordinary success stories? The answer is both simple and complex. You may have heard the adage, "Success occurs when preparedness meets opportunities." It's just that simple ... and it's just that complex. Extraordinary business leaders understand that opportunities abound, but only the prepared can capture the opportunities.

After reading this book, you will come to know that ordinary businesses are transformed into extraordinary businesses by effectively engaging in and committing to the fundamentals of growth-oriented thinking and strategic planning. Bottom line—high-performance businesspeople use strategic planning to shape and direct their growth.

What separates the leaders from the pack? The common thread shared by successful growth companies is that they are future-oriented—they have a clear vision of where they want to be and an effective strategic plan outlining how they will get there.

The Few, The Proud

The U.S. Marines set themselves apart in their advertisements by calling themselves "The Few, The Proud." They are proud that only a few can meet the rigor and possess the skills necessary to be a Marine. Many try and fail. Others won't try. Only a relatively few make it in.

Growth is much like joining the Marines. Growth can be elusive. A study of 3,700 companies conducted by the Corporate Strategy Board found that only 3 percent had unbroken growth for the period of 1990 to 1997. Moreover, less than 1 percent had sustained growth over the last 20 years. On the upside, those companies that were able to sustain growth literally doubled the return rates of the S&P 500 during the same time period—26 percent for the unbroken-growth companies versus 13 percent for the S&P companies.

Business magazines such as *Business Week, Inc.,* and *Entrepreneur* have annual lists of the fastest-growing businesses. Interestingly, however, many of the businesses that appear in the lists one year do not make the list the next. And a large percentage of the firms were off the list five years later. For a variety of reasons, they were not able to sustain the growth they had achieved earlier.

Going from ordinary to extraordinary is similar to winning a spot in an elite group, whether it be the Marines, a college basketball team, or a professional football team. Many try; few succeed. What does it take to succeed? Skills, determination, and a mind-set of winning. In a business setting, that mind-set is a focus on growth.

Our goal in writing this book is to help you achieve success in your business by getting you to focus on growth and on the strategic planning necessary to achieve that growth. Is it possible to grow without a strategic growth plan? Sure, it happens. Yet it is safe to say that developing a growth plan certainly increases the odds of success. We offer a straightforward and easy-to-follow approach—an approach that can make a difference for you and your business.

Why Every Business Needs to Plan

Recall that success occurs when preparedness meets opportunities. Opportunities provide great potential for wealth, yet opportunities are fleeting. An opportunity often presents itself for a short period of time and the business that can strike quickly is the one that reaps the rewards. This is the source of the phrase "window of opportunity." A window of opportunity is open for a short time and then closes.

Consider the low-carb diet fad that hit the country in the early 2000s. Experts predict that the fad will decline, and there is some evidence that it has already begun to wane. Yet, many companies hit this window of opportunity early and have made massive profits. Others—often those that were offering high-carb products—missed the window of opportunity and failed to adjust quickly to the changes.

So how do companies prepare themselves to move on these "windows of opportunity"? They have a plan.

In addition to helping business executives react to windows of opportunities, a strategic plan helps them overcome challenges from competitors and other aspects of the competitive landscape.

All businesses encounter challenges. Some businesses are victims of unfortunate and largely unpredictable environmental and competitive occurrences. Some simply miss their markets completely. However, most unsuccessful firms fall prey to their managers' lack of foresight. These leaders fall short of their potential because they do not properly analyze and evaluate their relative competitive strengths. They fall short because they lose their objectivity, becoming enamored with their products or services and failing to clearly read real market opportunities. They fall short because they are so out of touch with their markets that they don't perceive shifting consumer tastes and preferences. They fall short because they lack a clear blueprint of necessary goals and support activities and, thus, encounter costly duplications, overlaps, and internal inefficiencies. In short, these businesses miss being all that they could be because their owners and managers are unable or unwilling to focus on one of the prime determinants of business growth and success—planning!

Careful, strategic thinking and growth planning make a difference. When Roxanne Quimby met Burt Shavitz, Burt was a "reclusive beekeeper, … selling honey on the side of the road, … in gallon jars for 12 bucks."[2] This was certainly nothing out of the ordinary. In fact, Shavitz was the stereotypical small business.

The two teamed up in 1984 and began to expand, slowly and steadily. Concentrating on arts and crafts fairs, they sold honey in beehive-shaped jars that Quimby designed. They even ventured into selling beeswax candles. A good day could bring sales of $200—not exactly bustling growth and unbridled returns, certainly not extraordinary! But the idea was solid and the growth potential surprising.

By 1992, they were selling 500,000 beeswax candles a year and their expansion was just taking off. New products were added—beeswax lip balm, for example, proclaimed as the "world's best lip balm." All of these were logical, strategic extensions of their natural, beeswax base. Soon, they added moisturizing cream to their product mix. They expanded and relocated based on careful planning and consideration of bottom-line needs.

Today, this unlikely success story is known as Burt's Bees, a leading brand of natural personal-care products. Quimby, who sold 80 percent of the business in 2003 to an investment firm for $179 million, says it best: "Success doesn't come from one brilliant idea, but from a bunch of small decisions." A good strategic plan can show you the big picture and guide the way toward that "bunch of small decisions."

The evidence is solid. There is a clear and positive relationship between planning and organizational performance. And inadequate planning has reg-

Windows of opportunity are just that—they open and close quickly. A well-crafted strategic plan can allow you to take advantage of these open windows, leaving competitors in the dust, scratching their heads while trying to figure out why you won and they lost.

ularly been reported as one of the key causes or predictors of business failure. Stated simply, thorough and systematic planning can make the difference between being ordinary and being extraordinary.

Planning for Growth

Achieving growth and success is possible for any business, small or large, manufacturing or service, regardless of the dynamics of the industry. Successful growth does not play favorites. It is not reserved for only the most brilliant business minds. You can achieve growth if you pay attention to the world around you and your abilities to capture and exploit opportunities.

Growth-oriented thinking, and the planning it engenders, is not magical. It is easy in the sense that adopting a new mind-set is the key. You must change your mind-set from one of the status quo or day-to-day decision making to one of envisioning the future. It really is easy to change the way you think, but you have to consciously make that change, and you have to continue to practice growth-oriented thinking. You must train yourself to think in terms of growth possibilities whenever you observe or identify opportunities. You must learn to think in future terms.

Successful entrepreneurs have always been able to see opportunities that other people could not. They have always been able to step out of the mold, take some risks, and shape their destiny. Michael Dell started a mail order computer business in his University of Texas dorm room when everyone else thought computers had to be carefully programmed and installed by professionals. You can be the next person to break away from the pack. You need to challenge conventional thought in order to succeed. To pull away from the pack, you have to be willing to think beyond the present. You can't win by following the leader. You have to separate from the crowd.

Our approach to planning may force you to rethink or question what you assumed to be a given. Continuing to do something because "that's the way it has always been done before" isn't the type of thinking that gets you ahead. The "if it ain't broke, don't fix it" mentality isn't an option for top-performing businesses. If you are willing to shake things up and dig deep, the processes in this book can help you achieve significant success.

Why You Need This Book

This book is geared toward those of you who want to grow and expand your businesses. A growth-oriented business is one that is growing or is

You can achieve growth if you pay attention to the world around you and your abilities to capture and exploit opportunities.

poised for growth. The tasks that growth-oriented leaders like you face are far different from the tasks necessary to operate a business at current levels. Your needs are different. You have decided to stick your neck out and invest the time and effort to help your business perform better. Your quest for growth means constant change, and change demands planning. You face two key challenges.

First, as a manager of a growing business, you must be proactive. That is, you must direct your thinking and your team's thinking toward the future. You need to anticipate changes and make decisions about what is likely to occur. You must think in terms of anticipated changes in the competitive environment. You must think in terms of the financing necessary to reach new heights. You must think in terms of human and physical resources necessary to compete in the future. You must consider product and service development that will meet customer needs in the future. You need an effective strategic plan!

Second, you must create a culture of growth in your business. The culture in a growing business is different from that of other businesses. In high-performance businesses, growth is the focus; it is the topic of conversation in meetings and the discussion at coffee breaks. Managers and other employees discuss competition, the industry, and the economy as a matter of course. There is a different feel, a more upbeat and assertive approach to business. This type of culture doesn't magically appear. It starts with a plan!

The culture in a growing business is different from that of other businesses. In high-performance businesses, growth is the focus.

Consider the following example of a company that has made the transition from being a small business to becoming a growing business. Gary Erickson and Lisa Thomas owned a small business in Berkeley, California, called Kali's Sweets & Savories. It was a Greek-style bakery selling calzones and cookies to coffee shops and groceries. On a long bike ride in 1989, Erickson relied on PowerBars for nourishment. After overdosing on the PowerBars, he realized that they had the capacity at Kali's to produce similar bars from all-natural ingredients. So, Kali's introduced an all-natural cookie-like energy bar, the Clif Bar. As sales soared in the 1990s, the name of the business was changed to Clif Bar Inc. in 1997. LUNA bars were added to the mix in 1999. Though Clif Bar is still small compared with the firm that makes PowerBars, it has grown to be a leading maker of natural snack bars.[3]

The difference between Kali's Sweets & Savories, the local Greek-style bakery, and Clif Bar Inc. is one of focus. Kali's had to change its focus from a local market to a broader geographical market. It had to concentrate on the competition, on how to market the bar, and generally on how to grow.

In sum, it moved from being a small business to become a growing one that continues to grow and succeed. Why? Because it had a plan!

A Preview of What's to Come

Let's look for a moment here at the big picture for this book. In the next chapter, we spend time discussing why growth is good. Then we start the planning process. We start by setting the stage for planning—developing a plan to plan. We ask you then to peer into the future to get a glimpse of where you would like to take the company. But you can't just get from point A to point B without knowing about the potholes and chasms in your path. So we present the six faces of opportunities and the barriers to capturing those opportunities. We then ask you to take a deep, hard look at yourself, analyzing your own strengths and weaknesses and how those strengths can become competitive advantages. Finally, we take you to where the rubber meets the road—developing growth strategies for your company.

While not guaranteeing that you will become rich and famous by using our ideas, we are convinced that the planning roadmap we propose for you will make growth planning easier for you.

While not guaranteeing that you will become rich and famous by using our ideas, we are convinced that the planning roadmap we propose for you will make growth planning easier for you. We will point you along a path from being just an ordinary business to being an extraordinary business.

Notes

1. www.papajohns.com (accessed December 28, 2004).
2. Susan Donovan, "How I Did It: Roxanne Quimby," *Inc.*, January 1, 2004.
3. www.clifbar.com (accessed December 28, 2004) and Joseph Rosenbloom, "Follow the Leader," *Inc.*, October 1997, p. 83.

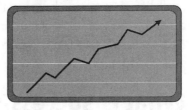

Chapter 2

The Road
to Success

AFTER EIGHT YEARS WITH TWO NETWORKING EQUIPMENT BUSINESSES, Mike Mendiburu was tired of the political shenanigans he'd encountered in the corporate world. When he started his own business in 1996, he wanted to keep it small, personal, and less complicated. There was nothing dramatic or particularly sexy about the business—High Point Solutions. They sold Internet-working hardware. They did not design the equipment, relying instead on the products of giants like Cisco, Lucent, and Nortel. Nor did they do installations, although they were willing to offer advice and support. Instead, though an extensive inventory of Internet-working products and the assurance of super-quick delivery, High Point maintained the networks of a small group of customers. They had their niche.[1]

Soon Mike was joined by his brother Tom and the business just kept growing. Focusing on a small group of clients, their reputation grew. Yet, even as sales soared, Mike wanted to keep the business small. Many of his employees were childhood friends. But High Point's reputation for dependability grew, and its client base expanded to include *Fortune* 100 companies. They had sales of $200,000 in their start-up year and sales of $60 million by 2000—nearly 30,000 percent growth in five years. Today, High Point still has a small company feel, and they are focused on doing business in a different way—keeping their commitments. Big companies, which can't afford Internet downtime, are banking on High Point. Mike and Tom Mendiburu and High Point Solutions have stepped from the ordinary to the extraordinary.

What Is Success?

Realistically, a business does not have to grow. Many entrepreneurs establish small, relatively stable niches and have no desire to go any further.

Success means different things to different people. For Mike Mendiburu, success had nothing to do with slugging it out and winning in a corporate power game. It had everything to do with becoming all that he wanted to be—growing, providing quality service, and doing it on his own highly principled terms.

We want you and your business to succeed. We want you to reach your goals and aspirations and feel satisfied that you've reached your potential.

Realistically, a business does not have to grow. Many entrepreneurs establish small, relatively stable niches and have no desire to go any further.

But you want more! Perhaps you're afraid that your niche is vulnerable as larger competitors enter your markets. Perhaps you see others taking risks, expanding their businesses, and reaping the rewards you know could have been yours. Perhaps you just feel that you're working so hard and so long, but moving in the wrong directions. There is hope, and it starts here as we consider the two foundations of this book, your road to success—growth and planning!

Gimme a "G"! Why Growth Is Hot

Growth is one of the hot topics in business today. But what's behind all the talk?

Why should you be so focused on pursuing growth? Why does growth make sense for you and your business? These are important and legitimate questions. We offer five basic reasons why growth is important for your business (Figure 2-1).[2]

Building the Bottom Line

Ultimately, all strategies are about building the bottom line. We choose strategies because we believe that they will lead to higher levels of profit for the business. Of course, there are two methods for addressing the bottom line game. You can try to *cut* your way to profitability or you can *grow* your way to success. Realistically, you probably do both. Yet, sooner or later, you

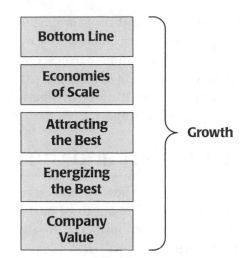

Figure 2-1. Five good reasons to grow your business

will face a decision like the one in the following example.

We recently worked with a midsized business that was experiencing some bumpy economic times. Their core business was steady but stagnant. The company's officers struggled with how to improve that all-important bottom line. Most of the officers favored cost-cutting methods. "Where and what can we cut?" became their message. Even downsizing was considered. The company's president took a different stand. He applauded meaningful cost control. But he believed that growth, not cost cutting, was the way to proceed. "You grow your way, not cut your way to success," he argued.

There is merit to both arguments. But here is the kicker. Many businesses are already running as lean as they can. Since there is no fat left in the business, further cuts will rip out needed muscle. If you are at this point, feeling that you've pared costs and cut back as much as you can, what else is left? How about the option of growth? There is more. Businesses that build the bottom line through growth tend to be able to sustain their profits over a longer period of time than businesses that generate profits through cutting costs. Growth becomes the vehicle for progress—the vehicle for building and sustaining the bottom line.

Businesses that build the bottom line through growth tend to be able to sustain their profits over a longer period of time than businesses that generate profits through cutting costs.

Realizing the Economies of Size

Growing the business results in a larger business. The larger the business, the more economies of scale you can realize. Economies of scale become important because they represent cost savings.

These savings come in a number of forms. For example, you may be able to get discounts by buying larger quantities of raw materials or components from your suppliers. You may gain efficiencies by having bigger facilities. As your company grows, production may be increased using capacity previously idle. Therefore, your per-unit costs will be lower. As you see, growing larger can have a bottom-line impact.

Attracting the Best and the Brightest

Growing businesses are able to attract the best and the brightest employees. The logic is basic. Good people want to be part of growing, winning organizations. They want to work for businesses that are looking to the future and focusing on opportunities.

Hewlett-Packard explains that growth helps attract and retain top people. In its corporate objectives, it states that high-caliber people "will align their future only with a company that offers them considerable opportunity for personal progress."

Energizing the Best and the Brightest

Now that you've attracted and hired the best and the brightest, what's next? You have to build a culture that energizes and builds commitment in your workforce. Today's employees desire opportunities for advancement. They desire challenge and appreciate the excitement of moving in new and innovative directions. They want to be part of successful businesses that search for and capitalize on new opportunities. They want to be proud of their business.

Many people contend that it is simply more fun to work for a growing business.

A growing business helps meet these needs. Growth opens avenues for promotion and advancement. Growth can be the lever of challenge and excitement that many workers need. There is a sense of life and energy as the business expands and progresses. Many people even contend that it is simply more fun to work for a growing business.

Strengthening Company Value

You may be surprised to learn that there is a clear relationship between business growth and company value. Faster-growing companies have higher profit-to-earning ratios than do their slower-growing counterparts. That probably makes sense. Slower-growing companies are often seen as being

12

less progressive and somewhat stale. Faster-growing companies are seen as being on the cutting edge. Accordingly, investors tend to place higher value on businesses that focus on growth.

The logic behind these perceptions is grounded in evidence. For example, one study showed that faster-growing companies yielded a 19 percent annual return to stockholders over a five-year period. In contrast, a comparable group of slower-growing companies produced an average return of about 5 percent over the same period. In short, business growth generates sales and profits that are critical for enhancing shareholder value.

You Have to Make It Happen

We are no doubt stating the obvious, but here goes. Business growth—with all its lure, attractiveness, and potential—does not just happen. You have to make it happen. You may have wonderful ideas, a solid feel for the market, and unbridled enthusiasm. But it's not enough. Great ideas, without careful plans, are like daydreams. They offer a brief escape, an emotional surge, and then they're gone—and reality sets in.

Planning, and more specifically strategic planning, is the mechanism or tool for shaping your growth ideas, refining them into marketable potential, and building a series of action steps to get it done.

Allow us to emphasize this point. We have worked with many business leaders who have been deluded by the "assumption of informality." It goes like this. "We need to grow, and we have a pretty good idea of where that growth needs to be focused. Let's get to work. We have a plan in our heads. Sure, it's just an informal plan. But that's good enough. We don't need a strategic plan, and we certainly don't want to take the time and energy to go through a detailed strategy process."

You may even be having similar thoughts. All we can share, based on years of experience with hundreds of businesses, is this: the assumption of informality rarely produces results. Instead, it leads to false starts, garbled communication, frustration, and uncertain direction. Often, employees in the business begin to question the leaders' competence and credibility. It just does not work. You need a plan. You need a strategic plan.

The Strategic Planning Buzz

Business guru Michael Porter has noted in *Competitive Strategy* that "the essence of formulating competitive strategy is relating a company to its envi-

There are two types of leaders in the world—dreamers and doers. The difference between them is that doers have a well-thought-out strategy to achieve their dreams. They possess a "dream it, do it" mentality.

ronment." We concur. Strategic planning is a powerful management tool for helping business leaders understand and respond to their environment. These two thrusts—understanding and responding—are the heart and soul of strategic planning. Of course, there is an additional and important complication. You are looking at the here and now, but you are also looking at the future. Successful strategic thinkers carefully anticipate what can be and create ways to make it happen.

Strategic planning begins with knowing your playing field and how that field is taking shape.

Strategic planning begins with knowing your playing field and how that field is taking shape. This is often referred to as understanding your business circumstances or, more formally, as understanding your environment.

Although we'll get more detailed later in the book, for now consider two critical environmental themes. You must know your customers and their preferences and tendencies, and you must know your competition and how it is likely to move.

This look at the environment allows you to recognize both solid business opportunities for growth and glaring threats that can stifle progress. This is the exciting, opportunity-oriented side of strategic planning that can be the spark for business growth.

But there is a very practical side to strategic planning. Armed with this environmental knowledge, strategic planning provides an overview and analysis of your business. It describes your firm's current condition. It helps you carefully assess key strengths of the business and identify real weaknesses that can affect the business and its competitive operation.

Finally, strategic planning prescribes an outline or action plan for how the business will proceed to capitalize on its strengths, capture the most promising opportunities, and minimize or mitigate its weaknesses and threats. This involves setting meaningful goals and building logical, well-reasoned approaches for meeting those goals.

This type of thinking and this approach to business is what strategic planning is all about. It makes a difference. For example, we are wowed by the success of Starbucks. With over 7,500 stores worldwide and revenues growing over 20 percent a year, Starbucks is neither average nor small. But consider the boldness of its early growth years.

Howard Shultz had a concept—a coffee bar. The concept was simple and was already a staple in many European countries—a place where people could meet to sit, talk, and enjoy a leisurely cup of quality coffee. Schultz believed it would work in the U.S. He further reasoned that people would be willing to pay a premium for the experience. As the concept evolved, Schultz continued to refine his unique angle: Starbucks became a meeting place, with comfortable chairs, couches, plug-ins for laptops—a place to meet clients and hold business meetings. Schultz knew his environment, anticipated potential angles for growth, and prescribed the way to get it done. He continues to do the same things today as the company surges forward with new growth initiatives. As one attorney noted, "A lawyer's eyes start to sparkle when he sees a person like Howard come in with a plan like Starbucks."[3]

What's in It for You?

It may be obvious that increases in the level and quality of planning are associated with better overall performance of the business. But let's examine in more detail some of the real benefits of strategic planning that you can expect to reap.

The overriding benefit is that strategic planning is a change-oriented process. Business owners and managers, like you, operate in a dynamic, volatile, and ever-changing environment. You must sift through, understand, and appropriately respond to the complex maze of rapid-fire changes you confront on a daily basis. Without sensing the pace and direction of change, environmental shifts can be overwhelming.

Strategic planning encourages a careful and systematic reading of shifts in technology, competitor position, and customer tastes. Further, the strategic planning process involves formulating actions to respond to these critical readings. As a result, change becomes a driving force of evolving strength rather than a jarring threat to stability. Consider the following example.

In an industry where similarly sized competitors have struggled or gone out of business at an alarming rate, Ross Marketing Services, Inc. has grown and prospered. To a large extent, that success has come from recognizing that its survival depended on strategically addressing the change within its industry.

In business for over 40 years, Ross has resisted the tendency of many advertising agencies to maintain their traditional, sole focus on the creative side of advertising. Ross reasoned that since graphic arts were rapidly becoming a computer-driven technology, a limited creative focus would be increasingly difficult to maintain competitively. Ross paid particular attention to changing customer needs and made the strategic commitment to transform the business to more fully meet those needs. Accordingly, Ross launched three new business units: Ross Training and Motivation (with serv-

Strategic planning encourages a careful and systematic reading of shifts in technology, competitor position, and customer tastes.

15

ices such as events marketing and sales promotion and training), Ross Lead Management (with services such as database management and lead generation programs), and Ross Custom Publishing (with services such as production art and technical writing).

These three new business areas, along with the core Ross Advertising, have enabled Ross to meet a broad array of customer demands and provide services it had previously subcontracted. Demonstrating true strategic thinking, Ross's leaders reason that looking at new technology and blending that technology to meet evolving customer needs will continue to be the formula for success.

Beyond the broad issue of change, strategic planning offers five specific benefits.

First, strategic planning helps you focus on the competitive nature of the firm. Externally, the plan encourages you to look at the competition, the economy, the community, and other key environmental factors to determine where your company fits. Internally, the plan forces you to assess the company's strengths and weaknesses. Indeed, this analysis may reveal hidden vulnerabilities or unique strengths. As a result, necessary changes in strategy can be made. Hopefully, initial planning efforts will foster the habit of periodically reassessing the firm's competitive position. In fact, one may argue that the process of carefully assessing the business and gaining an awareness of its potential and capacity may be as significant as the eventual plan that is derived from such an analysis.

The strategic planning orientation allows you to work in a "proactive mode"—looking to the future, anticipating, and planning for change.

A second benefit is that the strategic plan sets a formal direction for the business. It helps you determine where your business is going. In addition, and perhaps as important, it helps determine where the firm is not going. Thus, the plan helps you focus on specific objectives and stay there. This planning orientation allows you to work in a "proactive mode"—looking to the future, anticipating, and planning for change. As such, you can anticipate opportunities and position your business to benefit from them. Similarly, you can recognize impending threats and pursue decisive action to deal with them before disaster strikes. Thus, "crisis management" is replaced by a more fluid, logical, and systematic approach. Here, your management team understands and utilizes change as a competitive weapon rather than reacting to it as an uncontrollable nuisance to be ignored as long as economically and competitively possible.

The following example highlights the importance of the competitive awareness and focus benefits. An extremely enterprising young man possessed classic entrepreneurial flair. He was involved in three different business ventures and personally headed a firm that operated in such diverse areas as insurance, real estate, and managerial consulting. Not surprisingly, he was experiencing problems in nearly all phases of his business endeavors.

One might logically assume that the underlying cause of his difficulties was that he was attempting to do too much—spreading himself too thin. While this was occurring, this condition grew from a total disregard for formal planning activity. He failed to provide a clear view and direction for each business. No attempt was made to prescribe what needed to be accomplished, when, and by whom. Rather, he simply reacted and allocated his time and his firm's resources toward the most pressing problem of the day. Consequently, most efforts were stop-gap, temporary fixes that added little to the development of his firm. Additionally, he regularly missed important and potentially rewarding bids and contracts because his focus was on putting out yesterday's fires rather than looking toward tomorrow's opportunities.

Strategic planning helped this man understand his total business better and develop some concrete moves to enhance his competitive position. Additionally, since it was now clear what needed to be done, meaningful delegation was possible. Accordingly, he was free to concentrate on making contacts, meeting potential customers, and engaging in the necessary public relations work that he was uniquely qualified to perform. Thus, the firm realized and acted on important opportunities, and internal operations ran more smoothly.

The above example suggests a third benefit of strategic planning. As the firm's direction became clearer, employees were allowed to make decisions. They were allowed to utilize their skills more fully. They became more sure of themselves and comfortable in their roles and, accordingly, their jobs were enriched. You may have a similar situation. Most workers possess a strong desire to know what's going on and how their efforts contribute to the overall business objectives. Without a clear notion of these objectives, they cannot know, so they frequently become frustrated and dissatisfied. Thus, planning helps employees become part of the organizational team. As employees know more and more of what the owner has in mind, they will be more motivated, more willing to suggest ideas, and more willing to exert the extra effort needed to give the business an edge over competition. This is extremely important for your business. Employee input can often make the difference between success and failure. Indeed, as you clearly communicate direction, philosophy, and objectives to your workers, the returns are likely to be dramatic.

Fourth, a growth plan is useful to outside members of the board of directors or the advisory board. These outside people are not involved with the

A great benefit of strategic planning is that the process of writing the plan is repeatable. Therefore, once the strategic planning process is completed at the company level, each department or subgroup within your organization can create its own plan that ultimately feeds into the company-level strategic plan.

day-to-day operations of the firm. However, their job is to offer input and guidance to the owner. The plan provides them a basis for analyzing, evaluating, and offering suggestions for your company's overall operations.

Finally, the existence of a formal, overall, strategic plan makes the creation of special-purpose plans—such as financial business plans—much easier. In fact, the strategic plan contains most of the information used in developing more specialized plans. In short, although you may feel that planning is difficult and time-consuming, the planning process is overwhelmingly positive in its impact.

The Roadmap to Strategic Planning

Dwight D. Eisenhower once said, "I have always found that plans are useless, but planning is indispensable." While it may not be true that the strategic plan itself is nothing, it is true that planning is everything. Although it is important to have a written plan, it is the strategic planning process that is critically important for growth-oriented businesses.

Figure 2-2 highlights our strategic planning process. The process comprises three phases.

The *premise phase* occurs as you look toward the future and formulate a vision for your business. This phase also includes the development of a mission that provides a broad direction and philosophy for your business. We'll dig into this phase in more detail in Chapter 4. At the core of this phase are two important growth-related questions—what do you want to be and what can you be? It's important that you think neither too small nor too grandiose. You must be realistic, but also be a dreamer. If this sounds confusing, it truly can be. As we work through the premise phase, you will learn to stretch your thinking and strike the right balance.

During the *analysis phase*, you and your team will assess the key threats and opportunities in the business environment. This analysis requires concentration, not only on present environmental forces, but also on projecting trends and anticipating changes. You must not only identify and keep track of changes in key environmental factors, but also carefully assess or analyze the impact these forces and changes will have on the firm and its operations. Environmental analysis is therefore future-oriented, seeking to recognize the problems and potentials created for the firm by changes in its environment.

Whereas environmental analysis concentrates on forces external to the organization, internal firm analysis represents an evaluation of your firm's internal strengths and weaknesses. You will study a number of important internal issues as part of determining the strengths and weaknesses of the business. These will include assessing the financial status of the firm, analyzing human resource needs, studying market capabilities, and determining the ability of the company to produce a quality product or service.

Environmental and firm analysis enables the business to carefully and objectively portray both its special competencies and its relative competitive weaknesses. A distinctive competence is any area where the firm possesses a meaningful competitive edge over its competitors. Similarly, competitive weaknesses represent areas where the competitors' relative strengths are significant or overwhelming. Armed with this information, you can realize and capitalize on evolving competitive opportunities (competencies) and develop protective measures to minimize the harmful impact of materializing threats and obstacles (competitive weaknesses). Recognition of competencies and weakness enables you to choose broad strategies for dealing with these forces. The impact of distinctive competencies and competitive weaknesses is covered in Chapter 11.

After analyzing and evaluating environmental and company information and determining and delineating the firm's special competencies and competitive weaknesses, you are ready to embark on the *strategy development phase* of strategic planning. Here, you will use the results of the analysis information and assessments, consider the implications, and structure a working plan to guide the firm's activities.

The first step in the strategy development phase is to determine the overall growth strategy for the business. How much growth is desired? How will the business compete? What will be the primary strategic thrust in the near future? This step is a logical, functional, and integral process that can guide the firm along the path of success.

Once the overall growth strategy is established, you will then focus on more specific goals for the business. Setting achievable and measurable goals for the company as a whole and for operating areas is an important process.

The best strategies in the world are of limited value if they are not written. We will present and discuss a format for the written plan.

Figure 2-2 gives a sneak preview of the strategic plan format. As we move through the rest of the book, you may want to refer back to Figure 2-2 to see how the actions discussed fit into the final strategic planning document.

Often, when asking business leaders how much growth they want, we hear an all-too-common response—"As much as possible." Growing for the sake of growth, rather than growing to improve bottom-line performance, can be potentially devastating to a company. Controlled growth, defined as growth that improves bottom-line performance, is better than growing as fast as you can.

19

I. Creating a winning mission statement
    A. Product line or services provided
    B. Company vision
    C. Company philosophy and values
II. Identifying growth opportunities
    A. Broad-based environmental characteristics
    B. Industry-specific environmental characteristics
III. Evaluating company resources and capacities
IV. Determining distinctive competencies
V. Generating growth strategies and goals
    A. Company-level strategies
    B. Company goals
VI. Building target goals and target action plans

Figure 2-2. Strategic plan format

Help Is Good, But It's Your Game

Over the years, we have worked with a number of business owners and managers seeking to grow their firms. Quite commonly, one of their first steps was to find a consultant to lead them though the strategic planning process. There is nothing wrong with such an approach. It is important to find and use relevant expertise, and a good consultant can provide that talent.

Unfortunately, owners and managers tend all too frequently to yield the strategic planning process, as well as its outcomes, to a consultant. Remember: it is your business and your future that are on the line. You can use consultants for guidance and facilitation. A good consultant can help you think through the process and consider the range of issues that need to be addressed. Consultants can make recommendations and help you think through the impact of various actions. They should not make final decisions.

If you have decided to use a consultant, this book can be an invaluable guide as you choose and work with that consultant. Read the book thoroughly before your first meeting. You'll have a better idea of what questions to ask and a better perspective for appraising whether this is the right consultant for you and your business. Further, as the planning process proceeds, you will have a solid sense of where the consultant is headed. In short, this book can help you stay on course. If the consultant's direction appears to veer from what seems reasonable or desired, this book will give you a good perspective for discussing your needs and concerns.

Again, we reiterate—it's your business and your decisions that count; the consultant helps you develop and implement the best plan for you. Working with a consultant, just like working with any business partner, doesn't require less work. Instead, such a relationship demands that you've done your homework and have a solid awareness of the topic and a keen sense of when things are on the mark and when they are not. This book will help you address these needed sensitivities.

Notes

1. Susan Greco, "Little Big Company," *Inc.*, November 15, 2001, and www.highpoint.com (accessed August 14, 2001).
2. Based on an excerpt from Laurence G. Weinzimmer, *Fast Growth: How to Attain It, How to Sustain It* (Chicago: Dearborn Publishing, 2001).
3. Andy Serwer, "Hot Starbucks to Go," *Fortune*, Jan. 26, 2004.

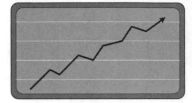

Chapter 3

The Plan to Plan: Let's Begin

S*UPPOSE YOU HAVE A CHRONIC DISEASE SUCH AS DIABETES OR HEART DIS-ease.* How would you like to have a nurse call you every couple weeks just to check on how you are doing and ask if you have questions or if your health has changed? If so, you would be a happy patient of American Healthways, #1 on the *Fortune Small Business* list of fastest-growing publicly held businesses for two years in a row.

American Healthways began as a diabetes management company, but it has branched out into other areas of chronic disease management. It is headquartered in Nashville and recently opened a call center in Baltimore. With earnings per share growth of 269 percent per year, it had earnings of $179 million in 2003. According to the company web site, "With more than 1.2 million lives under management, American Healthways is the nation's leading and largest provider of disease management, care enhancement, and high-risk health management services proven to improve the quality of health care and lower costs."

The basic concept for much of American Healthways' operations is that hospitalization can be reduced by earlier diagnosis of a change in a patient's chronic condition. Highly skilled registered nurses staff a call center from which patients are called with a frequency dependent on their condition. Patients can also call the call center whenever they need more information or think that their condition has changed significantly. This reduces unnecessary trips to the doctor and improves the health of the patient while reducing overall costs of health.

While you may not consistently grow at a 269 percent rate like American Healthways, every business can grow, and your business is no exception. If you have what it takes, you can make your business grow to new heights.

As you read Chapters 1 and 2, you should have developed some excitement about the value of growth and the possibilities that growth can bring. You should already be running ideas through your mind about how to achieve the growth you want, what the obstacles to growth are, and how you might gather information about new markets.

Before you jump into planning for growth, you should stop and make some very important decisions that can affect how you grow, how much you grow, and how fast you grow. The very first of these decisions is to ask yourself if you do, indeed, have what it takes to grow.

Do You Have What It Takes?

Before you jump into planning for growth, you should stop and make some very important decisions that can affect how you grow, how much you grow, and how fast you grow.

You already know that running a business takes a full commitment in order to run it well. You most likely are not spending great amounts of time on the golf course or the beach. Growing the business also requires full commitment of time, energy, and capital. You really have to ask yourself, "Do I want to grow? Do I want to work night and day to build this company? What am I willing to give up in order to build the growth I want to achieve in the coming year?" You may even want to stop here, lay the book down after marking your place, and go to the local Starbucks for a latte or take a walk around the block or just stare out the window for a while. Ask yourself carefully, "Do I have what it takes to grow? Do I want to change my life?"

Consider the decision to go international. Exporting products or services or setting up complete operations in a foreign country can reap really big rewards. But it cannot be done on a part-time basis. You must be psychologically ready to jump into exporting or you will fail. You have to work with the U.S. Department of Commerce to determine where good markets might be, and then you have to go look for yourself to make sure. Then you have to find out what changes in your products would be required to work in the foreign country. After that, you have to find a way to get the products to that market. Do you use an export management company? How about the logistics of transporting the product to the foreign market? These decisions can

23

take considerable time to flesh out and require a major commitment of your time. You can't really delegate this kind of decision.

Keep in mind that there is nothing wrong with staying small. As we mentioned in Chapter 1, there are millions of ordinary businesses. Their owners have decided that being ordinary is good enough for them. Committing the time, effort, and capital to get extraordinary growth is a major decision that must be made carefully. But if you want to grow, there is a big world out there, and there are opportunities to be captured. But you have to want it. You have to want it badly enough that you are willing to commit the time, effort, and resources to it.

If you are reading this book, you are most likely interested in achieving growth—moving to a higher level. You are interested in a higher-level market, a higher level of sales, or a higher level of profits.

How Fast Should You Grow?

There are three major factors affecting growth—the size of opportunities, the availability of resources, and the desire of the owner. Owners of growth-oriented businesses clearly need to plan. But before you begin the planning process, you may want to decide for yourself how much you really want to grow. For example, you may be somewhat conservative and risk-averse. You want growth, but you want to play it safe and not let growth get out of control. You must assess the environment you face to see what the limits of growth really are. Since you desire growth, you must watch the moves of your competitors. If your business is in retail or service, you must also watch the movement of customers. Similarly, if you desire growth, you must frequently be in touch with your financial backers to make sure that adequate funding will be available.

For owners of growing businesses, planning is critical. You must not only assess the size of the opportunity, but also determine how you can push the bounds of opportunity. In addition, owners of growing businesses must constantly plan for funding. Still further, owners of growing businesses must constantly plan for increasing production resources.

Consider the dotcom businesses in the 1990s. During that boom time, the high-tech businesses were growing as fast as possible, hiring workers as fast as possible, and expanding their facilities as fast as possible. When the dotcom crash hit in 2000, however, many of the companies spiraled downward into bankruptcy. In retrospect, most experts think that these failures were due to insufficient planning. Money was flowing easily, so owners reasoned that all they had to do was focus on raising capital. Unfortunately, their planning did not adequately assess the environment itself, the nature of the customers, and their ability to actually make a profit.

Setting the Stage for Planning

OK, let's assume that you've had your walk around the block, read a few more paragraphs, and decided that growth really is what you want for your business. Now it is time to get serious about planning for growth. It is time to develop a strategy edge using the model we suggested in Chapter 2.

But first, you need to set the stage. That is, you need to decide how the planning process is going to work for you. You need to decide who will be involved. You need to think about whether you need assistance from a facilitator or consultant. And you even need to decide whether you are going to change the entire direction of the company or make more minor tweaks to get growth going.

Who Will Be Involved?

It's your business. You own it or you manage it for someone else or you share in managing it with partners. Whatever the situation, you play a key role in deciding where the business is headed. With your decision to plan for growth, the first step is to determine who will be involved in the process.

Let's get past one tempting answer. It is tempting to say that you, the top decision maker, are the only person who needs to be involved. Lose that thought—now! Being a lone ranger is not smart when you are considering the complexity of strategic planning. It is somewhat akin to driving on a trip. As long as you are on the interstate and nothing out of the ordinary is going on, it is OK to do all the driving with no help. But once you are in unfamiliar territory and the traffic is snarled and the map is not clear, it helps to have others who help guide where you are going. In your business, if you are continuing the status quo and things are working smoothly, you can do it all by yourself. But once you move into uncharted territory because of the decision to grow, now you need help. Let's consider who would be likely candidates for the planning team.

Being a lone ranger is not smart when you are considering the complexity of strategic planning.

Certainly, you should be guiding the process. You should also include key managers of each of the functional areas or product lines. Thus, your team should include your marketing VP, the HR director, and the CFO or whoever makes financial analyses and decisions. If you run a manufacturing firm, then the operations manager or plant manager is a must. If you have product managers, they should also be involved. And you may want to add some key staff people who either can provide key information or would be directly affected by strategic change. This gives you a group of seven to ten key people in the company who are knowledgeable and who will be charged with implementing the new strategy.

We recommend erring on the too-large side rather than the too-small side. You can always break the planning group into subgroups with specific assignments. But having more individuals means that there will be more buy-in to the final plan and more communication throughout the organization. Erring on the too-small side can result in insufficient information gathering, groupthink, and the tendency to keep doing things the way they have always been done. It reduces the opportunities to hear from those who may have a different take on the environment the firm faces.

This does not mean that you should include everyone in the company. The group has to be manageable. It has to be small enough that meeting times can be found when few of the team members have conflicts.

The Players

Owner/President/Chief Executive Officer
All vice presidents
Product managers
If the company is small, key staff members
Members of board of directors, if appropriate
Administrative assistant for note taking and room administration

If the company has a board of directors—and any company considering growth should have—you should include key outside board members. This assumes that inside board members, those who are also employees of the company, are already on the planning team. Any employee who is respected enough to be on the board should certainly be included in the planning process. But what about the outside board members, those who are not currently employees of the company? This may depend on who those members are and what their time commitments are. In many cases, outside board members are currently running their own companies in addition to serving on the board of one or more other companies or not-for-profit organizations. Thus, they tend to be busy people. Expecting them to meet every Friday at 7:30 a.m. for months to do strategic planning is simply unrealistic. On the other hand, they may want to and be able to meet occasionally and be willing to communicate via e-mail or conference call to weigh in on important issues.

Consultants: Worth the Money?

As mentioned in Chapter 2, an issue in planning for growth is whether to hire a consultant or facilitator to guide the discussion and analysis. There is not a fixed answer to this question, but our experience is that a facilitator helps the team to explore new ideas while keeping the focus squarely on the topic at hand. The facilitator often brings a process—perhaps similar to our model in Chapter 2—that can show the team where its efforts should be centered at any given time. This keeps some members from wanting to jump immediately to strategy development without serious study of the firm's environment and its own capabilities.

Strategic consultants may cost anywhere from a few thousand to hundreds of thousands dollars, depending on the complexity of the task and the environment to be analyzed. It should also be clear that the consultant is just that, a consultant or facilitator. It is ultimately your responsibility to make the decisions. It is a grave error to bring in a consultant who waves a magic wand around for a few sessions and suddenly comes up with a grand strategy for the company. In this case, the key players on the team will have had little input into the plan and, hence, little buy-in to the result. Only when everyone on the team is on the same page does the process work well and end well.

Careful thought should be given to the hiring of a facilitator or consultant. Where do you find these professionals, and how do you know whether they are good or not? Many university business professors do strategic planning consulting for both large and small companies. There are also professional consultants whose only job is consulting with companies. There are other individuals who may work in the planning function in a larger company or even in not-for-profit organizations that may have significant experience in the planning process. In addition, there are industry-specific consultants who are experts in the particular industry that includes your business. For example, one owner of a growing company in the optical field routinely uses a consultant in that industry to help drive strategy. In another case, a bank may retain a consultant with banking industry experience to help make strategic decisions.

A key to finding a qualified consultant is asking around to see who has used which consultant. Consider interviewing potential consultants to see if you feel comfortable with them and their approach. Be sure to check with references. Ask about their approach. Ask how they price their services. Ask how long they recommend the planning process to be. Ask whether they prefer to stay on after the plan has been developed to oversee the implementation of the plan. By doing this preplanning homework, you can identify a consultant and establish rapport before the planning process actually starts.

How Often Should the Team Meet?

Often, the strategic planning process will require weekly meetings over a period of several months.

The strategic planning process is very involved and requires a substantial input of information and analysis. It is unrealistic to assume that a growth plan can be created in a couple meetings. Often, the strategic planning process will require weekly meetings over a period of several months. It is wise to have team members block out a 90-minute time frame on their calendars at a fixed time each week. Perhaps 7:30 Friday mornings for primary meetings with Wednesday lunch meetings for subcommittee meetings would work. Make sure up front that each member can accommodate that schedule. This is far better than simply saying, "We will try to meet some time each week." Let them know the importance of these meetings so team members will accept this time absolutely and keep to it without fail. Our experience is that early-morning meetings work better than late-day meetings, because it is so easy to let other meetings or priorities intrude into late-day times.

Planning Retreat Rules

Everyone must be there.
No skipping out at lunch.
Have an assistant there to be a gofer.
Have a working lunch—nothing heavy to induce sleep.
No cell phones or PDAs allowed!

Where to Meet?

Just as having a fixed time is important, it is also important to have a fixed place to meet. A good strategy is to have the initial meeting off-site for a half-day or full-day retreat. This allows you to spend some time explaining the need for the process, how the process will work, the length of the time commitment, and the final result of the process. It allows you to discuss the complexity of the firm's environment and the vision you have for the business. It allows you to get absolute buy-in to the process itself from each of the team members. This gives you the opportunity to introduce the facilitator and establish the facilitator's credentials. A period of time can be used to establish rapport between the group and the facilitator and among group members.

After the off-site retreat, regular meetings can be held in the corporate offices or a conference room. Again, block off the conference room on the company calendar to ensure that the same location is available every time the planning team meets.

A Well-Equipped Planning Room

Large conference table or small tables for four to six people with computer hook-ups

Really comfortable chairs (people will be sitting for many hours)

Ceiling-mounted projector connected to main computer

Refreshment bar

Conference telephone

Internet connection for main computer and individual laptops at tables

Dry-erase board with different-colored markers

Electronic marker board, connected to computer

Indirect lighting

Room to walk around (some people think better while pacing)

Explaining the Model

We have shown some of the tasks associated with setting the stage for the planning process. A remaining task is to explain the model we showed you in Chapter 2. This is an educational task for those on your team who have not done serious planning before. Flip back to the model at the end of Chapter 2. Convert it to a PowerPoint slide or draw it neatly on the marker board. You need to work through the model with your team before getting into the detail of each task.

Once you finish that, you are ready to start the process. You are ready to plan!

Behind the Scenes

As we discuss setting the stage for planning, it is useful to address what goes on outside the planning meeting. A key mistake is for planning committees or teams to meet weekly or biweekly and start each meeting with a review of what went on the previous meeting. This suggests that nothing goes on between the meetings and each team member begins each meeting trying to remember the thrust of the previous meeting.

Team members should each be tasked with assignments to complete before the next meeting. It may be to collect information about competitors that overlap with your company's products or services. It may be to formulate a draft mission or vision statement that can be used to generate discussion. It may be to access the latest auditor's report on the financial condition of the company. Alternatively, select a few members of the team to serve on a subcommittee to which a significant task is assigned.

And what about you? What should you be doing while your colleagues are doing their assigned tasks?

One recommendation is for you to think big picture. Try to anticipate where the team will lead in the next meeting. Take your walk around the block or kick back at a coffee shop by yourself to ponder where the company should be heading.

Alternatively, you can play the role of the integrator. In this case, you take the results of the previous meeting's discussion and put them in a summary form or a more readable version to discuss at the next meeting. Consider where there was agreement and where there was disagreement. Look at wording. Does the vision statement—as designed at the last meeting—really capture what you want it to be?

You are now ready to get into the actual planning process. We will lead you through a discussion of mission. Then you will look at three chapters each on how to discover the most about the world around your business and how it affects you. We then turn inward for three more chapters, looking at the company itself and how well it is poised to capture opportunities. When you are comfortable about both the outside and the inside, we then lead you through a discussion of competitive advantages and on to the development of strategies for growth.

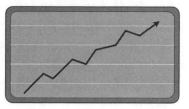

Chapter 4

Defining the Future

B Y 1997, PEPSICO HAD STRAYED SIGNIFICANTLY FROM ITS MISSION. Over the years, PepsiCo diversified into everything from fast-food chains to potato chips. The result—lost market share in its core business. In response, the company decided to spin off KFC, Pizza Hut, and Taco Bell to Tricon Global Restaurants, Inc. in order to focus exclusively on its mission:

> Our mission is to be the world's premier consumer products company focused on convenient foods and beverages. We seek to produce healthy financial rewards to investors as we provide opportunities for growth and enrichment to our employees, our business partners and the communities in which we operate. And in everything we do, we strive for honesty, fairness and integrity.

By refocusing on its mission, PepsiCo is now the market leader in the U.S. convenient food and beverage industry. In 2003, PepsiCo's market share (22 percent) doubled the market share of its biggest competitor, Coca-Cola (11 percent).

It's Like Pulling Teeth

Mission statements really do matter. But let's face it, if you want to make most businesspeople roll their eyes, just ask them to write a mission statement. It's a difficult and tedious task. Many times, after considerable effort, a company will end up with a very marginal mission statement, often full of meaningless jargon. Consequently, trying to get your management team to sit down and write a mission statement is like pulling teeth.

However, if you truly understand the purpose of a mission and its required elements, following the right process can enable any management team to create an effective mission. That is the purpose of this chapter.

Growing Up

A well-written mission statement sets up the framework for the entire planning process. It provides your company with strategic direction and discourages the "trying to be all things to all people" mentality.

When you were a kid, you would hear the same question from your parents, your teachers, and your high-school counselor, ... those ten dreaded words—"What do you want to be when you grow up?" It was a guaranteed source of stress every time it was asked. In this chapter, we ask the same question, only slightly modified: *What do you want your business to be when it grows up?*

If you ask most managers/owners of high-performing companies this question, they can immediately answer the question without blinking an eye. Moreover, if you asked multiple people in the same high-performing company that question, they would all come up with the exact same answer. Everyone would tell the same story.

Having a shared vision of where the company is going is essential in creating an effective plan for growth. Without it, a company may lose its strategic direction. Worse yet, it may find itself trying to "be all things to all people"—a surefire recipe for failure. Bottom line: an effective growth plan starts out with an effective mission statement. The mission statement sets up the framework for the entire planning process.

The Age-Old Debate: Vision Statement or Mission Statement?

Before we begin, let's clear up a common misunderstanding. There are many businesspeople who try to differentiate between vision statement and mission statement. They say that a vision statement is "what a company wants to be" and a mission statement is "what a company is today." These same "experts" also say that since vision and mission statements focus on different time frames, you need to separate them.

Interestingly, if you take a look at successful companies in almost any industry, you will find that they do not have separate mission and vision statements. Moreover, recall that we previously defined a mission statement as a tool that establishes "the framework for the entire planning process." Since the planning process is directed toward the future, the mission statement needs to be directed toward the future. Stated differently, a well-written mission takes the best of both worlds—it incorporates where we are today and where we want to go tomorrow.

A well-written mission takes the best of both worlds—it incorporates where we are today and where we want to go tomorrow.

Focus, Focus, Focus

A well-written mission statement can have a significant impact on a firm's ability to define its future. But what do we focus on? Where do we begin? If it is so difficult to write a good mission statement, how can we do it? Knowing the difference between *effectiveness* and *efficiency* is at the heart of it all.

So, what is the difference between effectiveness and efficiency? Here it is:

> Effectiveness is geared toward doing the *right* thing.
> Efficiency is geared toward doing things *right*.

The Easy Way Out

Unfortunately, when most managers set out to write a mission statement, they focus on efficiencies—trying to do things right. Efficiencies only consider how to improve at something you're already doing. It's an easy and relatively simple exercise. All you have to do is consider the activities that the company is already doing and see if there are ways to improve those activities. That's why many companies have poor missions. Moreover, the biggest danger with focusing on efficiencies is that the company may become really good at something, ... but it's the wrong thing.

For example, consider IBM Corp. back in the late 1980s. IBM became really efficient at adding high-tech bells-and-whistles onto all of its computers, continually pushing the envelope. As a matter of fact, IBM became better than any other competitor at doing so. Unfortunately, IBM became very good at doing the wrong thing. Customers didn't want bell-and-whistles on their computers; they wanted simplicity and a reasonable price. This allowed competitors like Dell and Gateway to enter the scene by doing the "right" thing. In retrospect, IBM became very good (efficient) at doing the wrong thing.

Making It Count

Conversely, good missions focus on effectiveness—doing the right thing. Defining the "right" thing can be very challenging. It's hard work and it may make your head spin. Questioning whether or not your business is currently doing the right thing is a difficult task. But the payoff is big. Have you ever known people who have made money seemingly in spite of themselves? Even though they may not know how to run a business efficiently, they may succeed because they have a really good idea or they may have benefited from being in the right place at the right time. These individuals aren't actually making money in spite of themselves; they are effective—even though they may not be very efficient.

If there is any one single outcome you must achieve from strategic planning, it is to ensure that your business is effective, that you are doing the right thing.

Here is a key takeaway. If there is any one single outcome you must achieve from strategic planning, it is to ensure that your business is effective, that you are doing the right thing. And only after you are confident that you are doing the right thing should you even consider doing things right (efficiencies). A well-written mission statement is the tool that successful companies use to ensure they are doing the right thing.

Mission Statement Basics

Some managers tend to write off or deemphasize establishing a strategic direction for their company, telling themselves that they already know where the firm is headed. But mission statements are among the most important considerations in the planning process. A firm's mission statement provides focus. Without such statements, a company may flounder, headed in no particular direction. The resulting confusion may not only stifle the progress of the business but also frustrate and demoralize employees.

The Future

Consider some household names like Sam Walton of Wal-Mart, J.W. Marriott of Marriott Hotels, Paul Galvin of Motorola, and Michael Dell of Dell Computers. Each started small businesses, but each had a vision of the future for a new product, service, or method of distribution. Their vision became the unifying force for their respective organizations.

Envisioning the future is a necessary ingredient for successful businesses. As the business environment becomes more and more complex, it is necessary for businesses to focus on the future so they will continue to meet the needs of an evolving market.

One of a Kind

The mission statement is a comment on the desirable and possible future state that a business will strive to attain. It should be crisp, clear, brief, and meaningful—not a set of platitudes. It should be unique to the particular business, and it should excite and energize people about the business and where it's headed. For example, consider the visionary comment that Boston Beer Company includes as part of its company mission: "We are committed to making Samuel Adams the largest and most respected high-end beer in the United States before 2010." Remember that missions need to be broad, yet clearly offer direction and focus for the business efforts of the firm.

Some may believe in a popular myth that business leaders are prone to have periodic flashes of brilliance, bringing them clear and inspirational business visions. While such revelations may occur on occasion, they are far from the norm. In most cases, leaders create their missions through careful study and thorough understanding of their business and their competition and by actively involving and listening to key constituents. Talking to customers, talking with employees, and questioning suppliers and vendors can all yield the kinds of perspectives needed to build meaningful missions. Straightforward inquiries—such as asking customers, "What would you like to see in a business like ours?" or "How can we better serve you and your needs?"—can provide key perspectives.

What Should It Look Like?

A mission statement is a concise statement of the general nature and direction of the company. By carefully delineating the underlying aim, scope, and direction of the business, the mission statement becomes an outline of what the company will do and what it will be. Although the mission statement is purposely broad, it must offer a clear word picture of the firm. Often, an elaborate, sweeping compilation of platitudes is offered as a mission statement. Such a statement fails to provide the precision and scope necessary to be useful as a meaningful planning tool. A challenging question that needs to be considered is "What separates us from similar companies?" The answer becomes a unique mission statement that is the basis for a definitive business strategy.

A well-written mission statement has two major values.

The first is as a communication, both inside and outside the firm. Naturally, the financial community will be interested in the direction the

A common question that inevitably arises is "How long should the mission statement be?" The length of a well-written mission statement should be one or two paragraphs that take up about a third to a half a page.

35

company is moving. But perhaps more important is internal communication. Often, employees complain that they never know what is happening. They don't know what management's plans are or how they, the employees, fit within those plans, which makes it difficult for them to be committed and motivated. The mission statement helps clarify the firm's vision and the employees' role in it.

The second major value is organizational commitment to the mission. If a concept or philosophy is believed strongly enough to put in writing, then everyone affected can expect that the idea will be followed. It's like New Year's resolutions, but with higher stakes. If you make resolutions but tell no one, there is no particular incentive to keep them. But if you write them down, ponder them, type them up, post them on the refrigerator, tell your friends about them, maybe even wager that you will keep them, this public commitment means you can't break them without losing face (or maybe money). In the same way, the written mission statement commits you to the stated strategy and philosophy and may result in equal commitment by others in and around the business. Such a commitment in no way suggests that a company's mission is cast in stone, never to be altered. A mission statement, as a representation of the firm's place in a dynamic environment, may change over time. However, such changes evolve as the firm assesses movements in its competitive situation. The mission statement provides a central focus and unifying drive for the business within its planning horizon.

The mission statement contains two major parts. Each should be given careful consideration.

The First Part of a Mission Statement

The first part of the mission statement defines and clearly specifies the basic nature of the business. Four areas must be considered:

1. The industry and product line of the company and customer needs that the company fulfills
2. Your position in the distribution channel (Are you a wholesaler, a manufacturer, a retailer, or a mail-order business?)
3. The prime goals of your company (quality, breadth of product line, price, or service)
4. Your target market (Who does the firm presently serve? Whom does it intend to serve in the relevant future?)

By telling explicitly what the firm is, the mission statement also tells implicitly what the firm is not. These limiting statements serve as a control to keep the general direction intact, similar to fences on either side of a highway. Consider the following example.

A woman decides to acquire a bicycle shop that sells and services bicycles. After a few months, she is offered the opportunity to add a line of mopeds. Reasoning that a moped is simply a bicycle with a small motor, she adds the line. Later, the regional manager for Honda motorcycles stops by. The local Honda dealer is retiring; this presents the shop owner a once-in-a-lifetime opportunity to land a coveted Honda dealership. Now she has a bicycle/moped/motorcycle business. Somewhat later, the entrepreneur gets the opportunity to take on a line of snowmobiles. Reasoning that snowmobiles really have much in common with motorcycles, except that they run primarily on skis instead of wheels, she adds this line too. The story could continue indefinitely as the woman adds garden tractors, lawnmowers, snowblowers, and so on. The point is that the one-time bicycle shop has become a highly diversified dealership for a number of slightly related products. In the process, the owner has overextended herself, is no longer able to do anything well, and has incurred substantial debt. In short, she has lost control of her operation. A well-written and closely observed mission statement would allow the owner to specialize in bicycles until she decided it was time to expand. Then she could carefully evaluate the market and her financial ability to take on an added line. Lines would be added at a controlled rate and with adequate financing.

By telling explicitly what the firm is, the mission statement also tells implicitly what the firm is not.

Many businesses, large and small, fail because of rapid, uncontrolled growth. For example, large businesses often acquire unrelated firms or start new businesses in unrelated areas with the stated goal of broadening their earnings base or gaining a countercyclical business. Many of these same subsidiaries are later divested as the parent firm's executives decide to "return to the things we do best." Obviously the corporation's management strayed from its basic mission and later realized its error.

The Second Part of a Mission Statement

The second major part of the mission statement is an expression of the firm's management philosophy, vision, and underlying values. Even though the mission statement by itself cannot create an organizational culture, it defines and espouses the kind of culture the company wants. Over the past dozen years, much has been written about "corporate culture" and its impact, power, and influence on the behavior and activities of large organizations. However, the concept of culture is important regardless of the size of an organization.

The mission statement should capture the company's basic philosophy of how business will be conducted.

The mission statement should capture the company's basic philosophy of how business will be conducted. In simplest terms, the mission statement should explain the core values that are most central and most critical to the business. The result is a value orientation that becomes an important guide for subsequent management action.

In making a philosophical or cultural declaration, the mission statement may say a great deal about the firm. Will the firm be a risk taker? Will it be employee-oriented? Will the firm be run according to the highest ethical standards? Will it be an aggressive competitor? Will it be a pioneer or a follower, a me-too firm? The key is to include those items about which management feels strongly and omit those items about which it does not. For example, the mission statement may mention nothing about a promote-from-within policy and instead discuss the strategy of hiring young managers with new ideas.

Increasingly, managers and executives are recognizing that while the formulation of the company mission is ultimately their responsibility, the process need not be an isolated activity. In fact, the formulation of a mission rarely comes from a flash of insight or inspiration. More typically, managers engage in a development process that involves input from numerous sources representing a range of stakeholders, including suppliers, customers, and employees. You will need to consider the significance and value of stakeholder input. In particular, employees at all levels often have important views and help guide and foster the mission's tone and direction.

Guidelines for Mission Statements

Patricia Jones and Larry Kahaner, in their excellent look at some of the best mission statements in the United States today, highlight a key starting rule or guideline: "Keep the statement simple." Simple doesn't always mean short, but it does always mean simple. Clarity and directness must be emphasized. Some businesses, such as Lowe's, are quite succinct: "Lowe's is in the business of providing products to help our customers build, improve, and enjoy their homes. Our goal is to outservice the competition and be our customers' 1st Choice Store for these products."

Also, be sure to have broad involvement in developing the mission. The mission will mean more and have a far greater motivational impact if those in the organization feel they have had a hand in crafting it.

In sum, the mission statement must do only two things, but it must do them well. First, it must set forth the direction of the business, thereby specifying what the business is and what it is not. Second, it must set forth the tone or culture of the business based on the owner's philosophy and vision of how the business should be run.

Dell Corporation

Dell's mission is to be the most successful computer company in the world at delivering the best customer experience in markets we serve.

Intel Corporation

Do a great job for our customers, employees and stockholders by being the preeminent building block supplier to the worldwide Internet economy.

Our Values: Customer Orientation, Results Orientation, Risk Taking, Great Place to Work, Quality, Discipline

Our Objectives: Extend silicon leadership, Deliver architectural innovation for convergence, Pursue opportunities worldwide

Walgreen

Walgreen's mission is to offer customers the best drugstore service in America. We are guided by a century-old tradition of fairness, trust and honestly as we continue to expand our store base and offer career opportunities to a fast-growing and diverse group of men and women. Our goal is to develop people who treat customers and each other—with respect and dignity. We will support these efforts with the most innovative retail thinking, services and technology. These success we achieve will allow us to reinvest in our future and build long-term financial security for our employees and our shareholders.

Federal Express

FedEx will produce superior financial returns for shareowners by providing high value-added supply chain, transportation, business and related information services through focused operating companies competing collectively, and managed collaboratively, under the respected FedEx brand. Customer requirements will be met in the highest quality manner appropriate to each market segment served. FedEx companies will strive to develop mutually rewarding relationships with employees, partners and suppliers. Safety will be the first consideration in all operations. All corporate activities will be conducted to the highest ethical and professional standards.

Figure 4-1. Winning mission statements

Putting It into Practice

The themes of this chapter present some important challenges. While we have built the case for crafting an effective mission, we have clearly noted the difficulty in attaining one. To initiate the process of crafting a mission statement, you will need to engage and guide the company's top-level managers to critically evaluate the business from an external or outside perspective. Rather than using an internal focus (considering what types of products/services the company offers), you will need to encourage managers to focus on who the customer is, the types of needs the company satisfies, and how the company satisfies those needs. By focusing on these three areas, you can ensure that the company will be using an external perspective to develop its mission statement. Too often a company will define its business simply by the products and/or services it offers. This internal approach usually provides too narrow a definition for the mission statement.

It may take a dozen iterations before your company settles on a mission statement. With each iteration, you may want to consider using different players to write it.

Finally, any company should be prepared to allow considerable time for the final mission statement to evolve. It may take several iterations before everyone is satisfied with the semantics of its mission statement. It can become a tedious process in which each word is analyzed and critiqued. This is perfectly acceptable. It is critical that the company be satisfied with each word because others will use the mission statement to guide them in developing future strategic plans.

Notes

1. Patricia Jones and Larry Kahaner, *Say It and Live It: The 50 Corporate Mission Statements That Hit the Mark* (New York: Currency, 1995), pp. 263-267.
2. Ibid., p. 157.

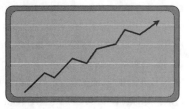

Chapter 5

Digging for Gold: Where to Look for Opportunity Information

COACH BEGAN OVER 50 YEARS AGO AS A FAMILY-RUN BUSINESS IN Manhattan, where quality leather goods were carefully crafted by skilled artisans. Adhering to the highest standards of material and workmanship, Coach has always focused on quality. In fact, the Coach handbag became the standard for fashion-conscious businesswomen. And then something happened. The mid-1990s brought signs of trouble. Same store sales were rocky and in some markets sales plunged dramatically.

Coach conducted consumer research in its U.S. markets and uncovered a threatening trend. Business casual was taking hold. Coach's products were seen as staid. Consumers began to turn to competitors such as Gucci and Kate Spade. As Coach's CEO Lew Frankfort noted, "They were beginning to capture the imagination of our classic user, ... particularly the younger consumer."[1] Coach responded. They rethought and carefully repositioned their product line. They began to offer accessories. They transformed their stores, making them brighter and lighter. Within five years, Coach had experienced a remarkable turnaround that saw compound annual sales growth of 25 percent.

Behind these numbers is thorough, ongoing research designed to ensure that Coach never again loses touch with its customers. Indeed, the firm's market research efforts are first-rate. Coach does phone interviews with 10,000 customers each year to stay apprised of their views of the Coach brand. At times, clerks are encouraged to question shoppers about the product and their preferences. Test marketing is now done in select stores before new products are rolled out to all 174 North American stores. Surveys and focus groups add to the informational mix. And the process is ongoing. Coach is committed to tapping the customer's thinking, delivering what the customer wants, and standing behind the product that is purchased.

The company is convinced that all this information is paying off. It is back in synch with its target customers, customers who are willing to pay a premium for the attention to detail that Coach offers.[2]

Why You Need to Do It

Many firms assess their strengths and weakness first and then attempt to identify opportunities based on their strengths. Successful growth companies make sure they understand market opportunities first and only then do they look inward at their strengths and weaknesses relative to market opportunities.

Strategic planning is an externally driven process. Monitoring the external environment signals what a firm does well and where it needs to improve. Rather than first analyzing its operations and then analyzing its environment, an effective organization will initially understand its external environment. Understanding environmental factors helps in forecasting future industry trends and directions. Understanding the environment must precede a constructive assessment of internal operations. In short, only after a complete external analysis is finished should a company begin to assess its internal operations.

Planning in today's dynamic environment may be the single most significant factor affecting a company's success or failure. Those of us who don't manage a *Fortune* 50 company must be particularly sensitive to environmental influences for three important reasons.

First, a growing company's responsiveness to environmental issues may be a source of considerable competitive strength. Your business can stay closer to the consumer than large multinational corporations can. By virtue of its smaller size, your firm can move with speed, flexibility, and sensitivity to accommodate shifts in customer preferences. Larger, more structured, and hierarchically bound organizations may be unable to change their direction or focus quickly. Consequently, flexibility can be used as a competitive edge against large firms.

Second, growing companies are particularly vulnerable to environmental influences. They cannot afford to misread their environment. Although one mistake or one misreading of a critical environmental trend may affect a large firm adversely, the error can usually be easily absorbed into the breadth of its total operations. However, a similar mistake may destroy a smaller business. Some businesses can't withstand such mistakes.

Third, growing companies usually don't have the resources needed to alter their environment; rather, they must respond to environmental changes. Therefore, it is imperative that management understand what is currently happening in its environment. In addition, successful companies must understand how their environments are changing. Therefore, it is necessary for them to recognize the major drivers that will affect the future of the industry.

Industry drivers are factors that shape the future of an industry in terms of both demand and competition.

Industry drivers are factors that shape the future of an industry in terms of both demand and competition. Managers of growing firms must have a good understanding of what drives their industries. For example, is the industry driven by government regulation? Is it driven by technological change? Is it driven by increasing needs for quality products? Is it driven by the imperative to control costs and offer products at lower prices? Is the industry affected by changing demographics? Obviously, there can be many environmental drivers. It is therefore necessary for successful managers to be able to identify key drivers in their respective industries.

The three reasons noted above—the benefits of smaller size, vulnerability to competition, and the need to identify changes in the industry—underscore the need for environmental analysis. A thorough environmental analysis is the difference between anticipating changes and reacting to whatever the environment presents. Which type of organization do you want to be? The choice is yours!

Proactive Thinking

One of the themes of this book is that planning stems from a proactive perspective. Simply stated, proactive managers look to the future and anticipate and plan for change. One reason for emphasizing environmental analysis so strongly is that it helps the business develop a proactive rather than reactive style of management. Proactive managers see opportunities on the horizon and position the business to benefit from them. Recall that in Chapter 1 we stated that "success occurs when preparedness meets opportunities." Proactive managers see opportunities that no one else sees and then are able to act on these "windows of opportunity" before they close. Moreover, proactive managers can also recognize impending threats and take actions to overcome them before disaster strikes.

In general, proactive companies outperform reactive companies. Even though there are risks associated with being proactive (aka the bleeding edge), in the long haul, the benefits outweigh the risks.

If your business is reactive, in contrast, it is driven by day-to-day demands. Events occur and the firm responds. A reactive business is always undergoing a new, usually unanticipated trauma. Crisis management is the modus operandi and putting out the largest fire is the focus of activities. In all likelihood, the business that fails to recognize and analyze its environment will become a victim of changes and forces within that environment.

Sketching the Environmental Landscape

Your environmental landscape establishes the context within which your company functions. The environment contains a set of factors that affect the business and its performance but that are external and largely beyond its control. When you perform an environmental analysis, you identify and examine key external factors and assess and evaluate the impact these factors will likely have on your company's operations and success. You analyze present forces and also attempt to project trends and anticipate changes. Environmental analysis is future-oriented—you seek to determine what problems and opportunities will likely be created by changes in the environment.

The process of analyzing the environment is illustrated schematically in Figure 5-1. The broadest set of variables comprises those technological, political/legal, social, demographic, economic, and global variables that may affect the business in only a general way. These variables make up the general or *macro* environment. A somewhat narrower set of variables that may have a more specific impact make up the industry environment. All of these variables tell us something about the dynamics of the industry and the players within it.

An Ongoing Commitment

Environmental and competitive analysis must be ongoing. Just as your firm's environment is continually in a state of flux and evolution, your analysis

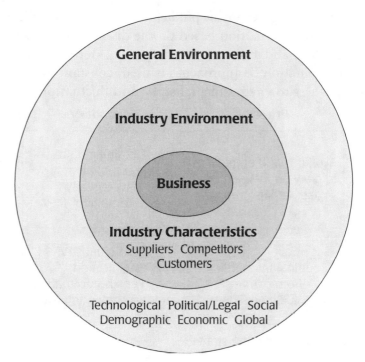

Figure 5-1. Understanding your environment

efforts must be similarly dynamic. When times get tough and your business is troubled, you may be tempted to turn your back on environmental analysis, arguing that you are confronted by too many pressing problems to spend the time and energy necessary to deal with environmental concerns. Such reasoning is dangerous and may serve to exacerbate an already difficult situation. How can you make the necessary decisions to reorient the business and adjust its strategic outlook without a keen awareness of its key environmental concerns? Environmental assessment and analysis form the basis for overcoming the firm's problems. Rather than being a time-consuming barrier, environmental analysis is a tool for corrective action.

Where to Go for Information

You may secure information necessary for environmental analysis from a number of sources. These may be secondary (existing) sources or such primary (original) sources as market research, customer interviews, or a study of competitors' products. Sources of information can also be distinguished as internal to the firm (for example, management expertise) or external to the firm (for example, government publications). Figure 5-2 illustrates four potential sources of information based on the distinctions between primary and secondary data and between internal and external data. Whichever approach or combination of approaches is used, constant awareness, monitoring, and openness to environmental shifts and fluctuations are critical.

	Primary	**Secondary**
Internal	Working with employees to draw on their expertise (e.g., brainstorming)	Obtaining data the company may have already (e.g., competitor files)
External	Collection of original information from markets (e.g., customer surveys)	Using industry publications (e.g., census information, trade journals, Internet)

Figure 5-2. Information-gathering strategies

Collecting Primary Internal Information

To identify the key environmental concerns most relevant to a business, it may be very beneficial to periodically engage these key employees in environmental brainstorming.

The first step in acquiring industry-level information is to meet with key employees. Specifically, certain employees spend every day of their working lives face to face with their external environment. Overlooking this potentially rich source of information could be extremely detrimental to gaining a comprehensive understanding of external factors.

To identify the key environmental concerns most relevant to a business, it may be very beneficial to periodically engage these key employees in environmental brainstorming—an open, freewheeling discussion that zeros in on the dynamics of a firm's particular environment. Brainstorming not only solicits important contributions from employees but is also an excellent vehicle for communication. Discussing the needs and direction of the business can foster understanding by and commitment from these key employees.

Questions about how often brainstorming meetings should be held, who should attend, and how long they should last are difficult to answer, but we'll offer some guidelines.

The timing of brainstorming sessions is dictated by the rate of change presently taking place in the industry. If your business is in a fairly stable industry with few contemplated changes, you can afford to meet less often. On the other hand, if your company is in a growing or evolving industry that is inundated with new forces, demands, technology, and competition, you will be forced to have more frequent sessions. At a minimum, these sessions should occur annually, with businesses in more volatile industries convening perhaps every six months.

Three to four hours should be allotted for such sessions. Once the program is in place, employees can do the necessary premeeting preparation on their own time, thereby shortening the meeting time. Initially, however, it is important to allow enough time for good, creative points to surface. As previously mentioned, participants should include all employees who have key contacts with the environment. For example, top sales or marketing people, financial managers, those who work closely with suppliers, and select members of the board of directors should share their comments.

Procedurally, an environmental brainstorming meeting can be run in a number of ways, although a fairly structured format is preferable, at least for the initial session. First, ask participants to list (independently) the key environmental threats and opportunities that they see for the business, both today and for the next year.

Reaching conclusions is not important at this stage. The object is to bring ideas and points for thought to the surface. It is probably best to accept everyone's suggestions without comment, waiting until later to reflect, analyze, and pare down the list.

Once participants have listed their opportunities and threats, they should rate each factor in terms of its impact on or significance to the firm. It probably isn't necessary to prescribe a detailed rating scheme; try asking participants to rate each factor as extremely significant, significant but not of the highest priority, or only mildly significant.

After all items have been rated, participants then present their ratings along with their justification or reasoning. Concentrate on commonalities—these will require little discussion. If everyone lists new competition as a key threat and assigns it the highest priority, then this factor clearly becomes an area of needed focus. If differences exist, participants should discuss them. For example, why does one participant consider suppliers a critical threat when no one else even lists this factor? Maybe this person knows something no one else does or perhaps he or she is off base. Nevertheless, the input and ensuing discussion are critical.

The process takes time, but it forces key personnel to become involved in the planning process and provides valuable information that may be unavailable or insufficiently detailed in historical analysis. The listing and rating that your team has just constructed, in conjunction with insights gained from historical data, identify the environmental factors the firm will attempt to track. Information about these factors needs to be constantly gathered and monitored. It is important that the business realize that environmental analysis is an ongoing task. Figure 5-3 provides an overview of guides to environmental brainstorming.

Area of Consideration	Explanation
Frequency of meetings?	Depends on industry At least annually More often for rapidly changing industries
Who should attend?	Key salespeople Key marketing people Key financial people Others with face-to-face contact with the outside Members of the board of directors
Preplanning?	Participants bring relevant data to meeting
Meeting dynamics?	Each participant shares information Participants identify opportunities and threats Participants rate/discuss opportunities and threats Commonalities are identified Priorities are established

Figure 5-3. Running an effective environmental brainstorming session

Collecting Primary External Information

Collection of primary external data consists of obtaining information directly from individuals outside the organization. It may include focus groups and interviews or surveys with suppliers, customers, and competitors. In addition, trade association meetings and conferences are often great sources of information. When deciding how to collect data, first consider what types of information should be drawn from the research. For example, let's assume you are interested in segmenting a customer market. A survey may be designed to measure how respondents rate several purchasing drivers (e.g., price, quality, serviceability, reputation, and delivery). In addition, the survey should identify demographic factors that may assist the researcher in segmenting the market (e.g., age, income level, education level, and gender). After the data are collected, the survey results may illustrate that people with one specific demographic background identify different purchasing drivers than people with another specific demographic background.

> When collecting primary data from external sources, be aware of the "squeaky wheel syndrome." Often, when hearing an outspoken customer in a focus group, managers will immediately react by making major changes. Unfortunately, the outspoken customer may not represent opinions consistent with any of the other customers and the changes are unnecessary. Make sure that the squeaky wheel doesn't get the oil unless it is warranted.

Collecting Secondary Internal Information

Secondary internal data are information the company has already collected and put on file. Asking managers for information they have collected about their industry and/or competitors may be very useful. Even if they are not sure whether certain data would be useful, it is still necessary to review the information.

Financial information—past annual reports, banking information, and financial investment plans—should be on file. This information can give good information about the company's condition, but it can also be used to look at to compare with other companies or the industry.

Collecting Secondary External Information

Secondary external information consists of existing documentation that can be found in most business libraries and on the Internet. Figure 5-4 provides a list of information sources for both general environmental factors (Chapter 6) and industry-specific factors (Chapter 7).

Factor	Sources
Technological	Technological Forecasts (PricewaterhouseCoopers) Predicasts Forecasts Industry Trade Associations and Journals
Legal	Industry Trade Association Reports and Journals www.nist.gov

Figure 5-4. Sources of information (continued on next page)

Factor	Sources
Social	Statistical Abstract of the United States Statistical Abstract of the World
Survey of Consumers	University of Michigan Institute for Social Research
Demographic	U.S. Bureau of Census Demographic Yearbook of the United States Statistical Yearbook Area Chamber of Commerce www.easidemographics.com www.census.gov
Economic	Economic Indicators World Fact Book Economic Report of the President Standard and Poor's Industry Surveys Census of Manufacturing/Retail Chamber of Commerce Reports www.bls.gov (accessed 9/30/04) www.census.gov
Global	Statistical Abstract of the World Management International Economic Intelligence Unit (EIU) National Trade Data Bank (NTDB)
Industry-Specific	Market Share Reporter Standard and Poor's Industry Surveys Industry Norms and Key Business Ratios Robert Morris Associates Census of Manufacturers industry Reports from Business Periodicals Trade Association Reports and Journals

Figure 5-4. Sources of information (continued)

Notes

1. Ellen Florian, "Six Lessons from the Fast Lane," *Fortune*, October 26, 2004, pp. 146-156.
2. www.coach.com (accessed October 26, 2004).

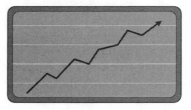

Chapter 6

The Six Forces of Opportunity

S O OFTEN WE HEAR OF "LUCKY" COMPANIES OR BUSINESSES. AT SOME point, all businesses will experience luck—some good and some bad. While some successful businesses may occasionally experience blind luck, so-called lucky firms are actually benefiting from a conscious effort to understand their external environments. There is little luck in business success. Remember: success usually occurs when preparedness meets opportunities, not through luck. And preparedness starts by developing a foundation based on a thorough understanding of broad-based environmental forces such as economic factors, governmental influence, technology, demographics, social factors, and globalization. These six environmental forces, as seen in Figure 6-1, may create significant growth opportunities for those companies that are prepared to leverage them.

Consider Andrew and Thomas Parkinson. They took advantage of two significant broad-based environmental trends: technology—the increasing use of home computers featuring user-friendly online services—and social factors—the decrease in leisure time among contemporary families. The result of capitalizing on these two broad-based environmental trends (technology and social factors) was a service for those whose time is perhaps more precious than money.

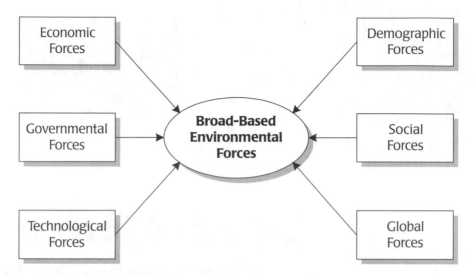

Economic Forces

Governmental Forces

Technological Forces

Broad-Based Environmental Forces

Demographic Forces

Social Forces

Global Forces

Figure 6-1. Opportunity forces

Peapod was launched back in 1989: the small start-up pioneered the online grocery delivery concept with just 400 households in a suburb of Chicago. As of 2004, Peapod (acquired by Royal Ahold in 2000) has grown to become the nation's leading Internet grocer, serving 155,000 customers in 13 U.S. markets annually, and has filled more than five million orders to date.

"The biggest hurdle was convincing consumers they could shop online and still maintain control over the quality of their picks," says Marc van Gelder, who joined the company from Ahold as president and CEO in 2000. "That's been Peapod's cornerstone all along. Today, customers see us for what we are: a lifestyle solution for their busy lives."[1]

Many outsiders may think that Peapod has been lucky (being in the right place at the right time). When taking a closer look at the company, however, it is easy to see that its success has come from having a solid understanding of the opportunity catalysts in its broad-based environment.

Understanding Broad-Based Environmental Forces

Every business is affected by the environment in which it operates. As highlighted in the last chapter, understanding a firm's environments is an important step in the planning process. Developing a comprehensive awareness of broad-based environmental forces will help you identify any external factors that could potentially impact the future of your organization.

In this chapter we restrict the firm's external analysis to the broad-based environment; industry-specific and competitive factors are discussed in Chapter 7. The broad-based environment comprises variables that are not company- or industry-specific but affect all firms, although each firm may feel their impact differently. As seen in Figure 6-1, six types of forces need to be considered: economic, governmental, technological, demographic, social, and global.

Economic Forces

Economic projections or forecasts are important. They affect your business, your industry, and your customers. Generally, economic information (at the national or state level) is readily available, although these data may provide only very general information rather than detailed economic information. Awareness of economic factors within your relevant markets becomes critical. For example, you may be concerned about factors such as trends in interest rates, unemployment levels, total sales, tax rates, and availability of capital. If your company is involved in consumer goods, changes in the level of disposable income may also become an important concern.

Consider the impact of economic conditions over the last few years. When the stock market transitioned from its long succession of bull years into a bear market, many industries were affected. Investors took a hit in the stock market, but it opened up opportunities in bond markets. Additionally, as the Fed lowered interest rates in an attempt to stimulate the economy, the real estate market was able to maintain significant momentum.

In addition, as a result of the 9/11 tragedy, we must now consider factors other than the Fed when assessing the economic environment. Certain industries, such as the passenger airline and hospitality industries, strongly felt the negative economic impact of 9/11. Other industries, such as segments of the aerospace and defense industry, have increased significantly from the tragedy.

Generally, economic information (at the national or state level) is readily available, although these data may provide only very general information.

Governmental Forces

Factors such as changes in government policy and regulations, legal developments, and changes in political philosophy may all affect your business. These changes can occur at the federal, state, and local levels. It is not unusual for social pressures to prompt enactment of legislative guidelines and requirements that affect business operations. For example, changes in health-care policy have had a dramatic impact on multiple industries, all the way from insurance companies to pharmaceuticals.

From time to time, tax laws change, with resulting effects on the structure and reporting practices. Consider the impact that the Enron scandal has had on every publicly traded company in the U.S. Now, financial reporting has become more closely scrutinized.

Pending judicial decisions that impact your business should be monitored closely. For example, deregulation in the airline, trucking, and banking industries has created tremendous growth opportunities for proactive businesses while threatening the future success of others. Recent deregulation of the utility industry has no doubt created the opportunity for proactive businesses, such as Ameren Corporation, to compete in markets that had been previously reserved for other utility providers.

Newspapers, chamber of commerce reports, trade publications, and general business publications (such as *Business Week* and *The Wall Street Journal*) are important information sources. Even more current information can be found through the many sources available on the Internet. Some computer users make a habit of checking the latest developments each morning. By reading and staying up-to-date on current and impending developments, managers can maintain a reasonably accurate appraisal of governmental trends and gain enough information to seek out appropriate professionals for more specific guidance when necessary.

Technological Forces

The presence and continued proliferation of computerized information is revolutionizing products, processes, and communications. Companies can now use flexible manufacturing systems to make customized products while simultaneously minimizing costs. Information management is becoming a source of competitive advantage in many industries. In 2004, 934 million people worldwide have been online, 1.17 billion will be online in 2005, 1.21 billion by 2006, and 1.35 billion by 2007.[2]

New technical processes are rapidly emerging and changing the nature and focus of organizational action. Key technological changes affecting your business and its industry should always be tracked. By following developments reported in trade literature, searching the Internet, and following reports of advances noted by suppliers or sales representatives, business managers may be reasonably aware of these key changes. Failure to monitor and address major technological innovations may cause a company to miss out on a significant growth opportunity. Moreover, it may adversely affect a firm's competitive position, particularly if competing firms use technical improvements.

Adopting technical improvements does not, of course, mean that every fad or innovation must be accepted. Rather, a careful analysis and systematic consideration of each advance is necessary to determine the potential effect on the firm, thus allowing the best and most relevant changes to be exploited. Further, a manager may avoid being caught in a position where customers perceive the business as being technologically backward or inferior to its competitors. If this occurs, a significant number of customers may be lost and the business may be forced to incur substantial expense to bring its technology up-to-date and online.

A few years ago, an insightful entrepreneur started a graphic design business. He had extensive experience in the industry, having been employed by his largest competitor for 14 years. Through his experience and exposure to the industry and his careful analysis of evolving trends, he concluded that all six firms in his selected target market were using outdated equipment and approaches. He felt that his business, by availing itself of the latest technological advances, could offer customers better quality at lower prices, thus attaining a competitive edge. He obviously was right. Today, all of his competitors are using cutting-edge software and other technology. The entrepreneur had gained a competitive edge by recognizing the trend and was able to capitalize on that edge for a period of time, which allowed him to gain a foothold in the market in spite of substantial competition.

Failure to monitor and address major technological innovations ... may adversely affect a firm's competitive position, particularly if competing firms use technical improvements.

Demographic Forces

Demographic factors are trends in population characteristics such as age, ethnic makeup, education, family composition, and gender distribution. The U.S. Census Bureau gathers and reports these data. Changes in demographic factors can have a significant impact on an emerging business, particularly if they indicate developing trends. Changes can affect either demand for a company's products or a company's ability to hire employees.

Demand Issues

Brinker International was founded in 1975. It has grown to over 1,400 restaurants worldwide, with 90,000 employees and system-wide sales exceeding $3 billion annually. The company has been referred to as the "mutual fund of casual dining," stemming from its "portfolio" of upscale, casual dining restaurants, which consists of Chili's Grill & Bar, Romano's Macaroni Grill, On The Border Mexican Grill & Cantina, Maggiano's Little Italy, Corner Bakery Cafe, Big Bowl Asian Kitchen, and Rockfish Seafood Grill.

Although many factors may help explain the performance of the restaurant company through the years, demographic factors may have had the most profound impact.

Although many factors may help explain the performance of the restaurant company through the years, demographic factors may have had the most profound impact. During the 1970s and 1980s, the United States experienced a critical shift in the dining-out experience, much of it a result of the demographic shift in changing family structures. First, there were more two-career couples, which explained the desire for eating out. But the attitude toward, and function of, dining out had also changed. Many families desired a place where they could sit comfortably for a moderately priced meal. Brinker realized that this was an untapped market. These were people who wanted neither the upscale dining experience nor the typical fast-food experience. The company created what has become known as the "casual dining experience," a combination of quality food with an enjoyable dining experience.

Today, however, maturing baby boomers are increasingly looking for upscale, casual dining. Restaurants with quality menus are reaping the benefits as more and more consumers reject fast food. This brings unique problems, however. With increasing demand for casual dining, the landscape has now become crowded with competitors. In response, specialty niches have become quite popular. Brinker International is capitalizing on this popularity. Several of the Brinker stable of restaurants—including On the Border Mexican Grill & Cantina, Big Bowl Asian Kitchen, and Rockfish Seafood Grill—fall into these niches.

> Baby boomers, those born between 1946 and 1964, constitute 72 million Americans, a group 40 percent larger than the groups born either before or after them. As the baby boomers approach their 60s, the demand for products and services catering to senior citizens will see dramatic growth. The new demand category, "aging boomers," has moved center stage.

Lest you think that baby boomers are the only group that should be considered, how about the next major market group—the millennials? This group, born after 1980, consists of 60 million people who are now in their teens and 20s. This group is only slightly smaller than the baby boomers and a significant force in the markets. Apparel, cell phones, and entertainment are some of the products that appeal to this "connected" generation.

One more example illustrates how demand for products or services changes as demographics change. With the U.S. population aging, many opportunities are arising. The demand for assisted-living facilities, for instance, is projected to grow at a rate of 30,000 beds a year. Senior citizens today are living far longer than earlier generations did; in fact, the single fastest-growing age group is people over 100 years old! And there is even a new category—the supercentenarians, people who are now 110. While large public companies will undoubtedly attempt to meet part of this demand, there is ample opportunity for numerous mid-sized companies to carve out special niches and succeed. Some companies, such as Del Webb's Sun Cities, are reaping huge benefits by offering general retirement communities to aging baby boomers. Additional opportunities may exist for businesses to focus on seniors with special needs, ranging from those who simply need help with household chores and shopping to those with Alzheimer's disease.

Labor Issues

As a growing business, one of the key issues you will face is getting the talent you need.

While demographics affect the demand for products and services, they also affect the ability of companies to hire qualified workers. As a growing business, one of the key issues you will face is getting the talent you need. Experts suggest that we are in the midst of a "talent force crisis." You may have experienced this. There are plenty of people who want jobs, but far too few who have the technical competence to be successful in the workplace. Millennials have not yet entered the permanent work force in great numbers. This leaves a gap between the needs of growing companies and the skilled workers who are available.

Growing businesses like yours have to figure out how to respond. Some businesses are looking for creative ways to keep their aging baby boomers. They are willing to offer flexible hours and shorter work weeks to maintain the skills that their businesses need. Many businesses have turned to temporary workers to give themselves flexibility in staffing.

Growth plans may have to be tempered if needed talent can't be found. Further, as the demand for labor increases and the supply of skilled labor decreases, wages are often bid up. This, too, can significantly affect the growth actions of many businesses. As you can see, the labor issue, which may become more threatening in the next decade or so as baby boomers begin to reach retirement age, can have pervasive effects.

Social Forces

Social forces are identified as the general attitudes, preferences, tastes, and beliefs of a society. One of the most visible social changes in the past couple of decades is health consciousness, a social trend that has influenced numerous industries. The dining industry, for example, has responded to health consciousness by offering healthier alternatives, such as a range of low-carbohydrate options. Some companies, such as Subway, have even built their entire marketing campaign around their low-carb alternatives. There are now even low-carbohydrate beers!

Consider both the positive and negative impact that health consciousness has had on the beef industry. About a decade ago, most popular diets required participants to decrease the amount of fat in their diets. Given the relative low-fat content of chicken, the poultry industry benefited significantly. Conversely, the beef industry saw a significant decrease in demand. For the first time in its history, the National Cattlemen's Beef Association (NCBA) was forced to aggressively advertise. Remember the series of "beef: it's what's for dinner" commercials attempting to promote the entire industry? Now, fast-forward to today. The low-carb diet plans encourage participants to eat high-protein foods such as beef. Bottom line, the same social factor, health consciousness, has created a major resurgence for the beef industry, because beef is high in protein and low in carbohydrates.

Another major social factor is convenience. As we have become a more convenience-oriented society, new business start-ups have benefited. Consider the coffee industry. At face value, most of us would have seen the coffee industry as mature and stagnant. However as we became a more convenience-oriented society, companies like Starbuck's Coffee, Caribou Coffee, and Java Hut have realized significant growth. These companies haven't prospered because society has an increased affinity for coffee. To the contrary, the coffee industry is mature and has experienced relatively low growth for decades. Moreover, premium coffees have been around for over a century. These companies have prospered because our society has placed a very strong emphasis on convenience. Convenient access to premium coffee is the social catalyst that created growth opportunities.

Another example is the spectacular growth of services aimed at the needs of working women. Currently, the majority of married women are working. At the same time, there is tremendous growth in single-parent households. These changes provide new opportunities for creative businesses. As work-

One of the most visible social changes in the past couple of decades is health consciousness, a social trend that has influenced numerous industries.

family conflicts have surfaced and moved to the social forefront, approaches for addressing and reducing those conflicts are begging for attention. In many cases, well-attuned businesses are etching out new competitive niches.

For example, KangaKab is a shuttle service that transports preschoolers to and from day care centers, filling in for parents whose hectic schedules prohibit the more traditional mom or dad shuttle. Youngsters and their parents depend on the white van with its navy-blue and mint-green logo to escort children to prearranged destinations between 7 a.m. and 5 p.m. on weekdays. During off-peak hours, KangaKab also transports groups of senior citizens to church, the movies, and senior centers. KangaKab franchises can now be found in more than 20 states across the U.S.

While poor assessment of social factors may mean lost opportunities, the stakes may get even higher. If you are blind to evolving changes in your industry, other companies will soon enter the market and fill the gap. On the other hand, if you monitor the environment, you can anticipate these changes and modify your business to leverage key opportunities. Then you can reduce the threat of potential competition and capitalize on an opportunity for expanding your revenue base.

Global Forces

Changes in the global environment offer tremendous opportunities and potential threats for businesses. Numerous high-growth businesses have realized significant benefits by either selling their products or services in foreign countries or importing raw materials in order to offer their products or services cost-effectively. The importance of assessing global markets has become increasingly important as a result of the development of satellite communication, cheaper and faster modes of transportation, the privatization of several overseas regions, and the emergence of economic alliances among countries.

The passage of the North American Free Trade Agreement (NAFTA) provides a significant opportunity for those U.S.-based emerging companies that can take advantage of more favorable export/import conditions with Canada and Mexico. While foreign markets may provide many opportunities, they may also expose your company to new risks. One potential risk is loss of domestic market share as a result of the emergence of foreign competition. Examples of U.S. industries that have suffered from foreign competition include automobiles, steel, and, most recently, overnight shipping.

Of the ten largest cities in the world, none are in the U.S. Which are larger than New York and Los Angeles? Shanghai, Mumbai (formerly Bombay), Buenos Aires, Moscow, Karachi, Delhi, Manila, Sao Paulo, Seoul, Istanbul, Mexico City, and Dhaka (formerly Dacca) are all larger.

59

One of the more recent developments in the global market that is having major repercussions in today's business is outsourcing. It began with outsourcing components to companies in Asia, where lower labor costs could bring down the overall cost of the components dramatically. Later, outsourcing of services such as inbound telemarketing has seen significant increases. Calls for service are often directed to India or Pakistan, where banks of phone workers answer questions or direct customers to higher-level answer desks. Buying airline reservations is another example where the customer service representative is not in Chicago or Dallas, but rather in New Delhi. Finally, even high-tech services are now being offered abroad. Medical diagnosis is beginning to be done overseas, with doctors reading patients' charts from the Internet.

Putting It into Practice

Environmental forces affect all businesses. The impact on growing businesses, however, is critical. Opportunities can come from demographics, from changes in the economy, or from new technological developments. For a growing business, don't forget to pay attention to the threats that you uncover. They can also be catalysts for growth opportunities. Search for ways that environmental threats can be turned into opportunities. Look at demographics, for example. The aging work force is a threat that certainly can affect most businesses. But that same aging population opens up significant markets that can pay tremendous rewards for the companies that take advantage of that population segment. Similarly, technological change can pose a threat as networked communications changes the way we do business. Those same changes, however, also open new markets and ways to attack existing markets.

Notes

1. www.peapod.com.
2. www.clickz.com/stats/.

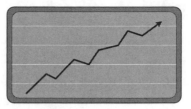

Chapter 7

The Playing Field: Assessing the Market

CHAPTER 6 DISCUSSED BROAD-BASED ENVIRONMENTAL FORCES THAT impact multiple industries. In this chapter, you will see a change in focus to the industry and competitive environment. Industry and competitive forces indicate whether an industry is growing or declining, who the major competitors are, what important supplier links exist, and issues regarding how customers define value. Developing a solid understanding of the issues is critical to high-performance organizations.

Just ask Michael Dell, CEO of Dell Inc. A little over a decade ago, Dell was a relatively small player in the computer industry, with annual revenues of around $500 million. Today the company has annual revenues in excess of $41 billion. How did they do it? Dell Inc. understands its customers' needs better than most of its competitors. In the 1990s, IBM Corp. was the dominant player in the personal computer industry. IBM believed that consumers wanted technologically complex computers. The more bells and whistles they put on their computers, the better. All of the other competitors in the industry were playing a game of follow-the-leader. So, as IBM products became more complex, so did most of the competitors' products. Unfortunately, all of these companies were focusing on what *they* thought was important, not what *customers* thought was important. Most customers didn't want technologically complex machines. Ironically, the more complex the machine, the more intimidated consumers became. Consumers didn't want complexity; they wanted simplicity.

Companies like Dell and Gateway understood their markets better than the market leaders. Consequently, while most computer manufacturers were following IBM, Dell focused on making computers easy and affordable. Dell succeeded and many of its competitors failed. Bottom line: Dell defined its playing field correctly, by understanding customer value, rather than relying on the market leader to pave the way for everyone else.

When most companies define the playing field, they define it based only on the competition. Successful growth companies realize there are many other factors that need to be considered.

Defining the Playing Field

You may struggle with the specific elements that should be included in your market analysis. Here, we examine five characteristics that need to be considered when identifying and assessing a market. Specifically, once the broad-based environment has been sufficiently examined, your analysis should turn to five factors: the general nature of the industry, its growth rate, dynamics of the competition, characteristics of consumers, and dependence on suppliers.

Industry Basics

You should consider whether product quality, distribution channels, changing consumer preferences, and product obsolescence are altering your industry. Understanding the nature of your industry gives you a feel for how successful particular strategies may be. Is your industry constantly updating and using state-of-the-art equipment or does it rely on existing equipment? Do customers in the industry demand high-quality products and service or are they willing to accept whatever is produced? Is the industry in a product market or a service market? Is it part of the consumer market or does it sell its products to intermediary firms? Are products manufactured totally within a single company or do subcontractors make components?

Incremental vs. Radical Changes

Industries generally change slowly. Incremental changes are based on improvements to existing knowledge or technology. Consider the computer hardware and software industries. Intel has made several improvements to the speed of its processors, including the 8088, 286, 386, 486, Pentium, Pentium II, Pentium III, and Pentium IV, and Microsoft has been successful with incremental improvements in its Windows, with 3.1, 95, 98, 2000, and XP.

Occasionally, an industry will experience a radical change, but radical changes are rare. When they do occur, however, they usually completely replace the need for existing products. The quartz watch completely replaced windup watches. Word processors have replaced typewriters. Advances in the Internet are replacing the need for many traditional marketing mediums. Many people today don't remember the mimeograph machines that were made obsolete by photocopiers. Mom-and-pop grocery stores essentially no longer exist. And while you should be able to anticipate incremental industry changes, radical changes are far more difficult to predict.

A firm competing in a high-growth market has far different opportunities and constraints than one that competes in a mature or declining market.

A firm competing in a high-growth market has far different opportunities and constraints than one that competes in a mature or declining market. In a growth environment, errors and inefficiencies can be tolerated. In a low-growth market with limited profits, errors can be fatal.

The concept of industry life cycle may be a useful analytical tool in examining an industry's growth rate. Typically, as noted in Figure 7-1, industries are seen as passing through four distinct developmental stages. The stage an industry is in affects the business because each stage is accompanied by a unique series of opportunities and difficulties.

For example, if a company's products are in the latter stages of the cycle (late maturity or decline), significant future problems may arise. This is particularly true if competitors are offering attractive alternative products and the business does not possess a strong market share. You may need to search for new products or reposition the business to deal with this threat.

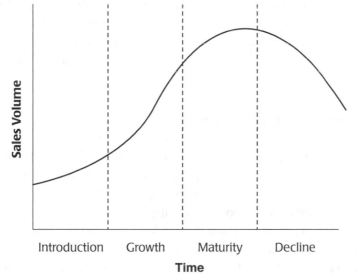

Figure 7-1. Stages of an industry life cycle

63

You should also understand how long it will take for products to move through the stages of the life cycle. Products may be approaching maturity, but if this stage is seen as lasting for a lengthy period, the impetus for immediate action is lessened. Similarly, relying too heavily on a product caught for too long in the introduction stage may adversely affect sales. Many factors, including the availability of substitutes and shifts in consumer tastes and preferences, will affect how fast the product moves through the stages. Failing to understand the level and extent of demand can result in harsh consequences. Identifying the current life-cycle position correctly and enacting a strategy consistent with these readings can be important factors of success.

Be careful not to pin your strategic dreams on a fad. You may make some quick money. But a fad, by definition, moves through the product life cycle quickly. It may have a quick up followed by a quick down.

The strategic impact of shifting life-cycle stages is demonstrated in the box below. Fitness, as a social trend, certainly was a theme that captured the 1980s and fueled the growth of related industries. But the obsession with fitness reached its peak by the latter part of the 1980s and began to decline. The decline seems to be across all age groups and therefore does not appear to be the result of an aging population. Americans seem to be moderating their exercise programs and focusing on relatively less strenuous activities, like walking, swimming, and biking. Manufacturers in fitness and related industries must realize they are likely to experience rapid life cycles. Typically, these product areas experience accelerated growth, early maturity, and speedy declines as fickle consumers change attitudes, interests, and leisure lifestyles at a dizzying pace. Rowing machines, aerobic videos, and perhaps even jogging accessories have felt the consequences of consumer fickleness.

The nature of industry capacity must also be addressed. If demand is strong but industry capacity is limited, businesses can take risks and exercise considerable flexibility. However, as industry capacity increases relative to demand, operational efficiency and cost control become critical and weaker firms are likely to be driven out of markets.

Sizing Up the Competition

One of the most critical parts of environmental analysis deals with competitive assessment. In many regards, the competition is the most commonly perceived threat an emerging business faces. For example, do the firms in the industry compete only indirectly and coexist peacefully or do they compete aggressively and attempt to drive each other from the marketplace? Is the competition price-based, quality-based, service-based, or a combination of all three?

Included in the dynamics of the competition is the relative size and market share. Some industries may be dominated by two or three major competitors.

New Balance Athletic Shoe, Inc.

In 1972 Jim Davis paid $100,000 to buy New Balance Athletic Shoe, Inc. This small shoe manufacturer had been in existence for over 60 years. Davis's purchase coincided perfectly with market demands, as the fitness industry in the U.S. was about to explode. As physical fitness became a national obsession in the 1980s, the athletic shoe industry experience growth rates as high as 20% annually.

While the market was experiencing double-digit growth, Davis's plan was basic—manufacture high-quality shoes as fast as possible to meet demand. The company basically played a game of follow-the-leader with Nike and Reebok. Unfortunately, New Balance followed the leaders as they expanded into a wide range of products. Lack of strategic focus left New Balance with insufficient level of product for its traditionally strong running shoe market. Moreover, the company had low brand awareness and limited marketing dollars.

By the early 1990s, the industry began to enter the mature phase of the life-cycle model. Slower demand created over capacity and a shakeout of some of the smaller players was inevitable.

Clearly, New Balance needed an effective strategy ASAP. Davis's response was to build on the business's traditional strengths and focus on a few tactical approaches. He called this strategy "Operation Quick Strike." First, New Balance created its own niche by focusing on width sizing. While other manufacturers offered limited sizes in terms of width, New Balance offered shoes ranging from AA to EEE. This product-offering strategy was difficult and expensive, but it gave New Balance an image of being a customized manufacturer.

Also, as industry sales began to decrease, New Balanced realized there was a huge demographic segment of the population that was transitioning from running to exercise walking. Operation Quick Strike also focused on increased advertising aimed at carefully selected targets stressing high-quality shoes that fit better than the competition. By combining a differentiated product and pursuing a fast-growing niche, New Balance was well positioned to succeed in a highly competitive market.

Today, Davis still runs New Balance and the company has positioned itself as the premier manufacturer of high-performance running shoes. New Balance has been the sponsor of the Chicago Marathon for the last eight years and is the sponsor of the Komen Race for the Cure series. Additionally, the company is the sponsor of past marathon world-record holders.[1]

It is extremely difficult for smaller companies to compete in such markets. Other industries are highly fragmented, with no dominant players. Still others may have a few national firms along with a number of smaller niche firms, such as the restaurant industry, where national chains compete along with locally owned restaurants. What is the role of franchises in the industry being considered? Independent businesses often have a difficult time competing with franchised units because of the name recognition and support provided by a national firm.

Recognizing and identifying competitors is no simple task. Competitors may take new forms as markets evolve and change. Customers' needs shift and are always being met in new and unique ways. Traditional businesses may encounter new types of competition that were not even considered in the past. Clearly, a growing business must be attuned to the changing face of competition. For example, you should consider the entry and impact of new competition in the industry. Who are these competitors? How will they affect the current structure and balance of the industry? What happens when an industry dominated by small independents must react to the entry of large national chains or franchises? In the latter situation, the independents must recognize that the entire composition of the industry has been radically affected and must make necessary adjustments.

Traditional businesses may encounter new types of competition that were not even considered in the past.

Initially, you should determine the number of competing firms and their market share in the trade area. Although a precise determination of market share may not be possible, collecting sales data of competing firms may provide a general understanding of relative market share. These data may be difficult to obtain, but simply looking on the Internet, opening up the Yellow Pages, or visiting the chamber of commerce should at least indicate the number of competitors. It is also important to assess the strengths, weaknesses, and unique competencies of competitors in addition to strategies they seem likely to use in the future.

One of the best ways to assess competitors and compare their strengths and weaknesses with one's own firm is to use a competitive analysis profile. This profile, done for each competitor, indicates and compares the key factors affecting each company's success. The factors chosen for consideration may vary, but the 15 factors listed in Figure 7-2 are typical. The comparison or rating need not be extensive or particularly sophisticated, but the analysis profile provides a clear snapshot of where each firm stands in terms of the 15 factors.

Knowing Your Customers

The customer target market is the set of individuals a business chooses to attract as its primary customers. A clear recognition of the needs, concerns,

Competitive Factors	Rating
Product/service uniqueness	
Relative product/service quality	
Price	
Service	
Availability	
Reputation	
Location	
Advertising/promotion	
Personnel	
Supply chain	
Financial health	
Production capability	
R&D competence	
Product/service depth	
Distribution	

Figure 7-2. Competitive rating example

and makeup of this group is critical because marketing and promotion are designed to appeal to a target market. Products and services are not ends in and of themselves. Many businesses forget this and become so enamored with their products or services that they fail to understand or see the customers' perspectives. Products or services, no matter how well conceived and developed, will be successful only if they meet some consumer need. Shifts in consumer tastes and preferences must be constantly monitored. Understanding the demographic and social makeup of the target market—specifically its distribution according to gender, age, marital status, income, occupation, and lifestyle—helps identify its needs and concerns. Shifts in target markets often offer new opportunities for a business. For example, a corporate investment advisor working with an aging population of workers may carve out a niche by focusing on low-risk retirement investments.

In addition, businesses must try to identify specific factors that impact consumers' purchasing decisions for their particular products or services. Are consumers more concerned with price, quality, service, availability, or reputation? A good understanding of the specific factors that drive consumers' purchasing decisions will allow your business to be more responsive to consumer needs.

Some companies have been able to differentiate their products or services so convincingly that customers are dependent on the business. Customers perceive that such products or services are unique and they can purchase them only from a specific company. For example, many avid golfers are convinced that they need the Pro V1 golf ball, which is produced only by Titleist. This gives Titleist great flexibility in both price and delivery.

Finally, you should assess whether any barriers to entry exist—that is, factors that discourage new companies from entering an industry. Tangible entry barriers may include capital requirements, access to information and/or distribution channels, and ownership of specific assets such as plant and equipment. Intangible entry barriers may include brand name recognition, intellectual property, customer loyalty, and company reputation. The combined impact of these entry barriers reduces the potential threat of new firms entering the market.

A good under-standing of the specific factors that drive consumers' purchasing decisions will allow your business to be more responsive to consumer needs.

Don't Forget About Suppliers

Often, companies focus all of their effort on customers and forget about knowing different players in the supply chain. Because it is important for you to keep abreast of suppliers and the factors affecting their success, you must consider your company's relationship to suppliers in light of two factors—dependency and vulnerability. Each business will differ, often considerably, in terms of these two factors.

Dependency refers to the extent to which a business depends on or requires extensive raw materials or subassemblies provided by suppliers. Some businesses are fairly self-contained and self-supporting, thereby exhibiting little dependency, whereas others are almost totally dependent on their suppliers.

Vulnerability refers to the extent to which a business would be affected by breakdowns in the supply network. Typically, business vulnerability is determined by the number of competing suppliers that could provide items for the business and the track record of these suppliers. In general, the fewer the sources of supply, the more vulnerable the business is to the actions of the suppliers.

Sometimes dependency and vulnerability issues surface over key customers rather then key suppliers. If, for example, a business is a captive supplier of a larger firm—that is, it sells nearly all of its products or services to one customer—then the business is extremely vulnerable when the larger firm encounters a strike or significant downturn. In most cases, the larger firm survives the trauma, but the smaller, dependent firm may not.

In considering high dependency and/or vulnerability, it is critical to be aware of forces that may affect the availability of raw materials or other components as well as their price and delivery. For example, a company that retailed specialized database marketing software established an extensive demand for its product through astute marketing to regional manufacturers and service professionals. The profitability of the firm, and indeed its survival, was threatened, however, because it had entered into an exclusive contract with a single supplier of its software, a small, fledgling operation located nearly 500 miles away. Unfortunately, as the software retailer grew and demand expanded, its supplier was unable to provide the needed updates. Extensive backlogs developed and customers, quite understandably, became frustrated. Before the software retailer was able to sever its relationship with the software developer and search out a more consistent source, customer confidence had eroded to the point that the business was doomed. Again, a careful analysis of the supplier and its capacity and ability to deliver, coupled with the firm's own projections of demand, should have enabled the software retailer to recognize this threat early enough to circumvent and overcome the disastrous implications. Again, the key is to proact rather than react.

Putting It All Together

We're now ready to look at the actual analysis. A threat-opportunity profile (TOP) can be a useful and beneficial tool. You should look at your company's environment to identify significant threats and opportunities.

As used here, a *threat* is any one of a range of factors that may limit, restrict, or impede the business in the pursuit of its goals. The presence of strong competition, changing public attitudes toward a firm's products, an adverse economic climate, and the bankruptcy of a key supplier are all examples of environmental factors that may pose threats for the business.

An *opportunity* is any factor that offers promise or potential for moving closer or more quickly toward a firm's goals. New high-growth markets, unmet or changing customer demands, the development of new products to complement existing lines, and a general upsurge in the local economy may all produce genuine opportunities for the business.

Deciding What to Consider

We all agree that it is important to carefully study historical data. But be careful. Some companies become so enamored with that data that they fail to look to the future. In the process, they miss opportunities for growth.

In conducting environmental analyses, you must decide which factors to track. For most businesses, it is totally unrealistic to believe that all the external factors that may have some influence on the firm can be studied constantly. There is neither the time nor the resources. Moreover, much environmental information is extraneous to a particular situation and therefore has negligible effects on the business. You must select the specific environmental factors that have the most critical impact on your firm—demand drivers and competitive drivers. These become the factors to track, study, and analyze. Although certain factors may be common to all firms, you will concentrate on a few key environmental factors particular to your situation.

One way to be sure which external factors are most important for your company, both today and in the near future, is to rely on historical trends. A careful examination of the past may reveal the environmental factors that have most critically affected the business and are relevant for future consideration.

In spite of the considerable merit and value to this approach, two problems exist in using historical evidence. First, these historical data may not be available because the variables may not have been monitored carefully in the past. Second, historical evidence may not be relevant to your future needs because the environment of a growing business is often rapidly changing and volatile.

It may be unrealistic and even dangerous to assume that past trends are indicative of future business conditions. Therefore, forward-oriented, insightful, proactive thinking may be lost if one adheres totally to historical trends. This does not imply that past records and trends don't provide meaningful and interesting input that should be considered. However, it implies that the firm needs to consider more than just historical records, to extend beyond these records. To the extent that it is available and relevant, historical information is valuable, but it is the beginning rather than the end of the analysis. Historical information is valuable to identify underlying trends. The difficulty in forecasting is attempting to assess the potential impact of general and industryspecific factors on the future of an industry.

Another caveat is that organizational success may foster an attitude of invincibility and prompt you to refrain from devoting the necessary energy to environmental analysis. In fact, your company's past success can be a formidable barrier to planning and change. An argument is often heard: "We've been doing it this way and we've been successful. Why should we change now?" Businesses with such an outlook are forced to change when the bottom line suddenly shows declining results. This doesn't mean that the business must always be in a state of flux; indeed, you may determine there's no need for change. But a decision not to change must be based on careful analysis and evaluation, not on complacency. If you continually assess, analyze, and interpret key environmental cues, the basis for decisions is grounded in thoughtful reason.

At the End of the Day

Driving forces are major factors that influence the future direction of an industry. A comprehensive analysis of an industry can yield an array of factors that may lead to future industry trends. However, only the most important of these factors will become driving forces for industry change.

A comprehensive analysis of an industry can yield an array of factors that may lead to future industry trends.

Two types of industry drivers exist: demand drivers and competitive drivers. Demand drivers are factors that affect future demand in the industry. For example, as we discussed earlier in this chapter, increasing health consciousness has created tremendous opportunities in health-related businesses. Health consciousness is therefore a demand driver. This same social characteristic—health consciousness—has had a substantial negative effect on demand in other industries. Consider the cigarette industry. As a result of increasing concern with health consciousness, not only are we smoking fewer cigarettes, but most public places are now designated as nonsmoking areas and California is a nonsmoking state. Clearly, increases in health consciousness have decreased demand in the cigarette industry.

Competitive drivers, the second type of industry driver, affect how companies within an industry compete. Take, for example, the stock brokerage industry. Until deregulation of the banking industry in 1987, stockbrokers competed only against other stockbrokers. Following banking industry deregulation, banks were allowed to sell stocks, which completely changed the nature of competition in the brokerage industry. More recently, technological developments providing Internet privacy through encryption programs have allowed discount brokers to change the nature of competition in the industry again by operating on the Internet.

The ultimate goal of an effective external analysis is to identify the major underlying drivers for the industry. The key word when identifying drivers is "major." Quite often analysts will use a "shotgun approach" in an attempt to cover any possible drivers. Some drivers may be extremely important to determining the future of the industry but others may have minimal impact. A good rule of thumb is to identify no more than three demand drivers and three competitive drivers. Limiting the number of drivers forces you to critically compare and contrast the relative importance of each one.

Note

1. www.newbalance.com (accessed October 8, 2004); Jay Finegan, "Surviving in the Nike/Reebok Jungle (New Balance Athletic Shoe, Inc.)," *Inc.*, May 1993.

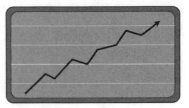

Chapter 8

Taking a Hard Look at Yourself

WINSPEC IS A MANUFACTURER OF CHIPS FOR ORIGINAL EQUIP-ment manufacturers of PCs. They began operations in 1997 in New York and now have facilities in California as well as in Taipei, Taiwan. Winspec has been listed among the fastest-growing companies for three years in a row by *Entrepreneur Magazine*. In spite of—or perhaps because of—their rapid growth, they have maintained excellence in the quality of their product. In fact, that quality is one of their strong suits.

By 1999 they had launched a fully spec-compliant branded module and had the goal of selling the highest-quality OEM module on the market. Five years later, they achieved that goal. Most of their chips are parametrically tested, using a verifiably better method of testing than that done by competitors. Their web site includes the following statement: "With a fully automated no operator involvement 'stencil printing through to reflow' we can guarantee 99.9 percent first pass yield which guarantees you a very low incidence of reworked modules, thus eliminating the possibility of field failures due to heat damaged components." This, in essence, guarantees no defects in their production.

Today, Winspec is a dynamic marketing company that combines a core technical expertise in technology deployment with a global business perspective. Winspec realized that quality was the key to their success. This insight has generated a steady stream of profitable revenue from its technology distribution and marketing activities.[1]

Once you have done a thorough study of the world around you, it is time to look inward. Like Winspec, you have to take a hard look at yourself to see if you have what it takes to capture opportunities in the marketplace.

The Value of Looking Inward

Taking a hard look at yourself is essential for at least two reasons.

First, many managers of growth-oriented businesses have inaccurate perceptions of their company's internal state of affairs. Often, they rely on personal opinion or "feel" to assess their firm's condition, which may result in an unrealistic perspective of the company's capacity, potential, and areas of concern. Only through a careful and systematic analysis can a reasonable and meaningful profile be obtained.

The second reason for doing an internal analysis is even more important. Essentially, looking inward reveals whether you have the means available for dealing with growth opportunities—a critical revelation. Having a good self-awareness can change the focus of your company's activities and strategies and can sometimes save the business from disaster. Yet for many companies and managers, it is a forgotten step in the logical planning sequence. Business managers tend to move strategically to capture opportunities without carefully considering their ability to do so successfully.

You must mesh your knowledge and insight about opportunities with a corresponding understanding of internal capabilities. Moving aggressively in the external environment without adequate internal support will, in many cases, lead to serious difficulties.

What Does It Take for a Self-Evaluation?

Analyzing and evaluating your own strengths and weaknesses requires time and commitment. It's not unusual for companies to spend several weeks analyzing their strengths and weaknesses. In a way, it is more difficult to study your own organization than to study the environment you face. Much of the information you gathered about the economy, the industry, and the competition is already published. It is there for the taking. You have to look at it, study it, and analyze it carefully, but the information is generally available and it is relatively believable. Information about your own company, how-

One of the most prevalent causes of failure among growth companies is trying to capture a growing opportunity without sufficient resources. Only when we match opportunities with strong capabilities in the company can we expect success.

ever, may actually be more difficult to find and it may be biased.

Consider marketing strategies, for example. It may be easy to assess how many dollars have gone into a recent marketing campaign. Determining how effective it was may be far more difficult. Other aspects of a company, such as employee morale and willingness to change, may be difficult to assess correctly. And sometimes, depending on how the information was collected, the information may be downright wrong. Even financial results that should be easily understandable may be elusive because of the variety of variables that could be used to determine financial ratios.

Thus, it is important for you to be just as objective about internal information as you are with external information. It is critical for you to be on the lookout for any biases in the analysis that may creep into your assessment of the company's ability to compete and grow.

Here is a final caveat before we get into the details of this hard look at your company's competitive abilities. You may have noticed the placement of these three chapters *after* the three chapters on the search for opportunities. It was intentional. We want you to look outside first; then look inside. By looking outside first, you know what the growth opportunities are and how easy it may be to achieve the level of growth desired. Now, when you look inside, you have a context, a perspective, a sense of what is really needed to achieve growth. You can now look very objectively at your own situation to see how well you can capture the opportunities.

If you study your own situation in a vacuum, you only know the absolute values for whatever it is you are studying. But if you have looked outside first and then study your own capabilities, you have both an absolute assessment and relative assessment of where you are heading. It makes much more sense to know information in relative terms than in just absolute terms.

Company Strengths and Weaknesses

One of the most basic, yet insightful approaches to your self-assessment focuses on the identification of strengths and weaknesses. As the terms are used here, a strength is any resource or capability that helps the business realize its objectives and strategies, capitalize on its opportunities, or defend against its threats. Conversely, a weakness is any factor that hinders the business from realizing its objectives and strategies or capitalizing on its opportunities or that leaves the company vulnerable to competition.

One of the most basic, yet insightful approaches to your self-assessment focuses on the identification of strengths and weaknesses.

Let's take strengths and weaknesses a bit further. A strength is anything that helps us realize our goals. But strengths can lie along a continuum from just being something we do OK to something that we do extremely well. A significant strength is something that we do exceptionally well, both from an absolute sense and from a competitive sense. It is something we can exploit. It is something that *other companies* try to emulate, because they see how successful we are. Similarly, weaknesses are things that we don't do well. They are parts of the business where things just don't click right or we are weak. Like strengths, weaknesses can fall along a continuum from areas where we are perhaps just average to areas where we are especially vulnerable to competition. We call these latter areas *strong weaknesses.*

Now, let's go one more step. We look at our operations—our financial situation, our marketing skills, production issues, human resources, and others. We can analyze these areas of the company from the viewpoint of day-to-day operations. But for our purposes, it is more important to look from a strategic perspective. That is, are we poised to successfully implement the strategies that we develop? Consider the following analogy.

You probably go see your family doctor to get an annual physical. In that case, you are going to your doctor to get an assessment of your general health condition. Now, suppose you decide to train for a marathon. Now you go to your doctor to get a pretraining physical. Your physician will now look at you from the perspective of how you could perform under great stress. This exam is different from the routine physical. In the same way, you do annual and quarterly financial reports that tell you the general health of your company. But you need to look more carefully at the company—studying it in more depth—if you are planning for growth.

Venture capitalists do this all the time. If an entrepreneur submits a business plan to a venture capitalist, the odds are very good that the VC will reject the plan out of hand for a number of reasons. But let's assume that you submit a proposal to a venture capital firm and it makes the first cut. The VC will then enter what we call a *due diligence* phase. That means they will carefully analyze the company from the perspective of what is necessary to achieve the rapid growth that venture capitalists require. They will certainly look at the markets, as we suggested in the past few chapters. But they will focus on the strength of the management team, the availability of patented products or processes, the amount of capital needed compared with the amount already available, the amount of ownership they will require in order to invest, and the length of time before they can cash out.

Painting with Broad Strokes First

A painter, starting with a blank canvas, first envisions what the scope of the painting will be. Broad strokes are made to set the tone for the painting. Once the basic outline is formed, possibly even by drawing with pencil first, more detail is added. Finally, a thin brush is used to fill in the minutest detail—the eyelashes on a child or the individual leaves on a tree. Each layer of detail drives the next. Adding a blue dress for a young girl then leads the artist to add complementing colors for buttons, jewelry, or scarves.

No company is strong in every part of the operation. Find those areas where you have great strengths and exploit them to every extent possible.

Analyzing a company's strengths and weaknesses is similar to this. We start by making broad brushstrokes about how the company is doing. These broad strokes then lead us to more detail where needed. A broad brush shows that our financial condition has some problems. We then zero in on that to determine what factors may contribute to those problems. We then zoom in further to ask why accounts receivable are running too high. We can then look at individual buyers if necessary to determine why those particular buyers are not paying us on time.

Figure 8-1 shows a broad-brush analysis tool. We start with it to identify where we have significant strengths or vulnerabilities. Then we get into the next task of determining just why we have those specific strengths or those specific weaknesses.

The broad-brush areas we suggest are the categories of financial condition, marketing capabilities, operational efficiency, and human resources. Keep in mind that the categories chosen and the variables analyzed may differ depending on the type of company and industry involved.

Using the Broad Brush

Consider how to use the broad-brush tool. You may want to start by scanning in the table and converting it to a handout or slide for use in a group discussion. Here is how to use it.

Step 1

First, identify key areas for your company similar to what we have done here. Look for factors that can be measured and that have at least some relevance for your company's growth plans. If you are working in a group, you may even want to brainstorm to see what areas or factors are worthy of analyzing. In order to keep people focused on identifying variables without pre-

Area for Analysis	Strategic Significance	Strong Weakness	Slight Weakness	Neutral	Slight Strength	Strong Strength
Financial Resources Overall performance Ability to raise capital Cash position						
Marketing Resources Market share Knowledge of markets Location Product quality Promotion Pricing Distribution						
Operational Resources Facilities Access to suppliers Inventory control Organizational structure						
Human Resources Number of employees Top management abilities Right mix of employees Compensation Employee morale						

Figure 8-1. The broad-brush analysis

analyzing them, present only the first column (areas for analysis) or first two columns (areas for analysis and strategic significance). Rate the strategic significance on a 1-10 scale, with 10 being critical and 1 being not strategically important. For now, keep all factors on your list, regardless of their rating. You can come back later and eliminate those with low scores. Once you have 20-25 variables identified, along with their strategic significance, you can go to step 2—analyzing the factors.

Step 2

Give each internal factor or resource examined one of five ratings: strong weakness, slight weakness, neutral, slight strength, or strong strength. Clearly, degrees of strength and weakness exist. Each factor or resource must be assessed and weighted as being slight, neutral, or strong. Scores for some variables—such as financial ratios, defective-product rates, or labor turnover data—may be readily available, because industry standards exist for comparison purposes. In other cases, objective data are often unavailable. You may want to know the effectiveness of advertising, but have no figures relating sales to advertising efforts, so you use a judgmental approach. Here, estimates will be sufficient for the broad brush analysis. More detail can be captured later to build confidence and objectivity into these judgments.

You or your team should try to assess as closely as possible whether each of the variables is a strong strength, a strength, neutral, a weakness, or a strong weakness. Spend considerable time in this exercise. It is worth your time. You may even want each member of your team to analyze and rate each variable independently. Then, bring the group back together to compare notes. Where do you agree? Where do you disagree? Why? Is there a consensus? If so, come up with a final rating for each of the variables. You may even find that you really do not know some important variables. If so, how will you find that information? What measurement will you use to determine if the variable is indeed a strength or a weakness? You may even want to form a subcommittee whose assignment will be to bring objective information about a variable or factor to the next meeting. Make them bring solid evidence to back up their contention that the variable constitutes a strength.

There is a reason why this is so important. We all think we have a good feel for how our areas of responsibility are doing. But we have often gleaned that over time and our assessment is often a subjective and intuitive rather than unbiased and objective. Urging your people to bring evidence of an

You or your team should try to assess as closely as possible whether each of the variables is a strong strength, a strength, neutral, a weakness, or a strong weakness.

assessment—whether good or bad—requires them to be more objective and answer the inevitable "why" question. Why is something good? Why is it bad? Is it strong in an absolute sense or in comparison with competitors or over time? Why are we better or worse than our competitors?

Step 3

By now, you should have a list of variables, an estimate of each variable's strategic significance, and a consensus value for its relative strength or weakness. Put the finished table on a dry erase board, an electronic slide, or other media where changes can be made for all to see. Now step back and look at your work.

Circle or highlight those factors whose strategic significance is low. Now circle or highlight those factors that scored a neutral on the rating scale. Look at these carefully for a minute. Are they important? From a strategic viewpoint? If they are, perhaps you should raise the strategic significance. If not, erase them! If the variables are not significant from a strategic standpoint, we need not consider them any more, even if they are a strong strength or a strong weakness. Those variables may, indeed, need attention and should be corrected if they are weak. But they do not need our *strategic* attention. The exception to this is where you have a variable or factor that rates a strong strength and could become strategically significant if you want it to. Here, you look at this area carefully to see if there is some way that you could exploit that strength.

> Are you being totally objective in your analysis? Everyone likes good news and we tend to focus on those things where we look good. But we tend to ignore those things where we don't look so good or to rationalize that those items are not really important anyway. Force yourself to be totally objective.

Now look at the variables that received a neutral rating. Erase them, too! Why, you ask? Why erase those variables that rated relatively high for strategic significance, regardless of the strength rating? Shouldn't we be concerned about those factors that are strategically significant? The answer is a resounding "Maybe!" But not now. And here is why. If we are neither really good nor really bad at something, it is not likely that we will ever move to really good or really bad. It certainly is not likely that we can ever exploit that variable. At the same time, we are good enough that we are probably not going to be thrashed by competitors on that factor. Certainly, we need to keep a watch on these variables because they are, indeed, strategically significant. But we do not need to give them the in-depth, analytical analysis that we are going to give other variables on our list.

Now look at what is left. You should have a list of 10-20 variables that are both strategically significant *and* either a strength or a weakness. And some of these will be both strategically significant and a *strong strength* or a *strong weakness*. These are the variables that command our detailed attention, our objective analysis, and our resource investments.

The Good, the Bad, and the Ugly

The factors you have selected are strategically significant and either good or bad. In either case, more analysis is necessary. If a factor is a strategic weakness, this means that it is something that your competitors could exploit. Even without that, the weakness will keep you from achieving the growth you want. You have to give attention to this factor. You have to delve more deeply to see just how bad the factor is. Suppose the variable you are looking at is your debt ratio. This may be strategically significant. But what does a high debt ratio mean to you? It means that the odds are good that you will not be able to acquire even more debt to underwrite your growth. It likely means that you will have to go to equity markets to get the capital you need.

If a factor is a strategic weakness, this means that it is something that your competitors could exploit.

Now consider the good. Here you have a factor or aspect of the company that is both strategically important and ranked as a strong strength. Again, you need to study this aspect of your company closely to make sure that it is, indeed, a strength. If it is, you can exploit it in pursuing the growth you desire. Suppose, for example, that you have an excellent distribution system for your current products. If you are considering growth by bringing out new products, your existing distribution system can be used to maximize the success of your new product entry into the market.

Recall that we suggested ignoring those items that were just average or neutral for the company. Suppose the distribution system we mentioned above was only average. That is, it is meeting the needs of current products, but perhaps just barely. Now if you want to add a new product to your market mix, you have to consider the impact on the distribution system. Can the existing system be used to market or distribute the new product in addition to current products? Perhaps, but we may not be able to depend upon it. So it is not an exploitable strength. Sooner or later distribution will have to be addressed, but currently we do not see it as either a key to our strategy or a vulnerability that can keep us from achieving our goal.

How about the ugly? The ugly is made of those variables or factors for which we just don't have good information. What information we have is fuzzy at best. Perhaps one of your managers insists that the variable being considered is a strong strength, but can't really substantiate it. We have probably all been in that situation. We are just sure that our area is doing well and any failures by our area or the company as a whole are someone else's fault. This discussion can get ugly as others press us to "put your money where your mouth is." We may protest that there may not be any way to objectively know for sure, but we intuitively just know that we are doing well. And the discussion goes on and on.

The ugly is made of those variables or factors for which we just don't have good information.

Moving to a Finer Brush

You have now painted a company profile with a broad brush. It is time now to start refining the analysis to learn more about the company's ability to grow. It is necessary to analyze your company's strengths and weaknesses with a fine tool in order to understand how the company can compete and grow. We need to drill into the data to get more precise information about the company's current position as well as how it can fare in a growth mode. For example, cash flow is often a problem for companies that have a seasonal or cyclical market. Adding to that the need for cash to underwrite growth means that significantly greater amounts of cash must be accessed. So it is imperative that we have accurate information about the flow of cash into and out of the company.

Similarly, human resources must be analyzed carefully if the firm intends to grow. Sometimes tasks can be outsourced to others, but many aspects of the company's operations must be done in-house. In particular, additional management-level workers will be needed to guide expansion. You must plan accordingly.

We proceed now to two chapters dealing with the more precise level of analysis. Chapter 9 will show you how to take a hard look at the financial aspects of the business and Chapter 10 will follow up with hard look at marketing, operations, and human resource issues. We then bring the discussion of the business environment together with these three chapters and discuss distinctive competencies—how our strengths compare with those of our competitors as we consider opportunities.

Note

1. "Heat Wave," *Entrepreneur* Magazine, June 2004, p. 64.

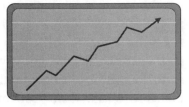

Chapter 9

Running
the Numbers

ADVANCED NEUROMODULATION SYSTEMS (ANS) IS THE EIGHTH-fastest-growing small publicly held company in the U.S., according to *Fortune Small Business* magazine. It designs, develops, manufactures, and markets implantable neuromodulation for chronic back pain or nervous system disorders. The company markets three principal product lines: the Renew radio frequency system, the Genesis and GenesisXP implantable pulse generator (IPG) systems, and the AccuRx implantable drug pump. For the six months ended June 2004, revenues rose 36 percent to $57.1 million and net income rose 50 percent to $8.3 million. Its three-year average earnings per share growth was 131 percent. Revenues reflected increased unit sales of Genesis and GenesisXP implantable spinal cord stimulation systems and Renew radio frequency SCS system. Net income benefited from improved gross margins.

Neuromodulation devices include implantable neurostimulation devices, which deliver electric current directly to targeted nerves, and implantable drug pumps, which deliver small, precisely controlled doses of drugs directly to targeted sites within the body. The company's products utilize technologies that offer advanced programming features, user-friendly interfaces, and smaller implanted devices, resulting in greater patient comfort. ANS markets its products to physicians who specialize in managing chronic pain.

83

ANS's 52-week-high stock price was $48.29; its low was $24.85. Its price/earnings ratio was 40.65, compared with the industry's 31.40. Its beta—an indicator of its market risk—was 1.18, suggesting a slightly higher than normal risk. However, it carried no long-term debt and its quick ratio—an indicator of liquidity—was 14.58, indicating that ANS likely had plenty of cash, if not too much, lying around. However, further analysis would show that the company had just issued additional stock the previous year and was gearing up for additional growth.

Financial Resource Analysis

In a growing firm, financial resources are probably the most critical key to its growth strategy.

In a new business, adequate financial resources often mean the difference between success and failure. In a growing firm, financial resources are probably the most critical key to its growth strategy. For example, excellent growth opportunities may be identified along with reasonable strategies for capitalizing on them. But without adequate financial resources, the strategies may lay dormant for years, never to be implemented. Even more disturbing, a business may be forced to halt a viable project or program in midstream after its financial capacity has been exhausted. Analyzing financial resources can help identify such problems and prevent such disappointing occurrences.

Problems uncovered in the financial analysis may catch the manager's attention. The problems may be in marketing, inventory control, purchasing, pricing, or perhaps even human resources. But the problems eventually show up in financial performance. Therefore, the financial analysis becomes the most obvious starting point.

As you begin to examine and rate the relative strength of your financial resources, certain caveats must be kept in mind. Existing financial statements should be used as tools in the evaluation process; they rely on historical data and thus are pictures of past behavior. It is reasonable to assume that past behavior can indicate present capacity and future expectations. Yet, if your company is in a growth mode, these figures may not capture the firm's vitality or future prospects.

Rapid growth in an industry dictates that firms continuously invest capital to keep up with the demand for their products. This means that growth businesses will often be in a weak financial condition. Their financial condition may be far more questionable than the condition of a similar business that is not encountering growth. For example, many growth-oriented businesses go public without ever having made a profit. But their potential for growth is so great that investors are willing to infuse cash into the business.

In addition, financial analysis is only as powerful as the extent and quality of the information on which it is based. If you have gathered little meaningful data or have prepared scant and limited financial statements, it becomes much more difficult to draw worthwhile financial conclusions. It is imperative, therefore, that you do your homework and create financial reports that provide accurate information.

Many managers find it useful to compare their financial picture against some general standard. Understandably, they want to know how they stack up against their industry's performance norms. Such comparisons can be useful barometers or checkpoints for the business, but must be approached with some degree of caution. Financial ratios, for example, may be significantly higher or lower than comparative standards yet have a perfectly plausible explanation. Therefore, comparisons are only one way to assess the company's financial condition.

Comparative financial information may come from a variety of sources. Dun and Bradstreet publishes *Industry Norms and Key Business Ratios*, the Risk Management Association (known as Robert Morris Associates until 2000) publishes *Annual Statement Studies*, and Leo Troy publishes the *Almanac of Business and Industrial Financial Ratios*. Each covers a vast number of industries, typically further broken down by company asset size and sales. Additional comparative information may be obtained from trade associations, trade magazines, annual reports of publicly held competitors, and other sources specifically related to particular industries.

Financial analysis is only as powerful as the extent and quality of the information on which it is based.

Reading the Numbers and Between the Lines

Three financial statements are key to understanding the financial condition of your business. It is imperative that you understand the statements and the ratios that are derived from them. Without this knowledge, you are little better than the blind men feeling parts of an elephant; each has a different interpretation of the elephant because they touched the trunk, the tail, or the leg. If you have the three financial statements, but do not understand how they relate, you too will have different interpretations of your financial condition.

Analyzing the balance sheet, the income statement, and the cash flow statement is an important first step in analyzing the financial health of a company. They are especially useful when presented both in dollars and in percentages and compared over a period of several years. Although changes are never easy to assess, the comparative statements can be quite useful when studied specifically to determine the causes of change.

The following tables (Figures 9-1, 9-2, and 9-3) show the income statement, cash flow statement, and balance sheet for Advanced Neuromodulation Systems, which we discussed in the opening vignette to this chapter. We will use ANS throughout this discussion as an example of how financial statements can show a wealth of information. (These statements are for discussion purposes only and are not to be construed as either good or bad financial condition or company management.)

As we discussed in the opening vignette, ANS manufactures and distributes implantable devices for control of chronic pain and other diseases. Its customers include neurosurgeons, anesthesiologists, and orthopedic surgeons. Headquartered in Plano, Texas, it went public in 1981. Let's see what we can learn from just a cursory glance at the three statements.

From the income statement (also called a *profit and loss statement*), we see that ANS's revenues jumped 81 percent from 1994 to 1995, significantly declined in 1997, rebounded nicely until incurring a 20 percent drop in 2000, followed by three years of over 50 percent growth. The overall growth for the 10 years was 550 percent. Its growth in operating incomes for 2001, 2002, and 2003 averaged 155 percent. Thus, aside from a couple of down years (1997 and 2000), ANS showed significant growth.

From the cash flow statement, we have that free cash flows have had their ups and downs, with the most recent being a $2.4 million negative cash flow in 2003, but still leaving the company with a healthy $8.5 million in cash and no long-term debt. Note also the significant numbers in 2002 in the cash flow statement from investments and financing. Their financing brought in $84.9 million, primarily from a stock offering. The cash flow from investments shows a negative $91.1 million, meaning an outflow of over $90 million. Where did it go? ANS's annual report sheds light on that.

To position the company for sustained, profitable growth, ANS has made significant investments in product development, intellectual property, marketing resources, organizational capabilities, manufacturing capacity, systems, and processes. These investments are the building blocks that will promote and support future growth. In 2003, we began construction for a new headquarters, acquired our remaining domestic distributors, increased spending for new product development, added 150 new associates throughout the organization, and acquired the exclusive rights to new applications for our technology. ANS has made these important investments while maintaining the planning, execution, and leadership discipline to deliver on our financial commitments. Simply stated, we have invested heavily in our future while continuing to drive strong revenue and profit growth, and we plan to carry the same strategy into the new year.[1]

This is also shown in the balance sheet. Look at PP&E (Property, Plant and Equipment). Note that this figure changed from $10.6 million in 2002 to $21.1 million in 2003. This figure is likely to change more in 2004. Note also on the balance sheet that the category "Short-Term Investments" jumped from $2.2 million in 2001 to $85.8 in 2002. This is the rest of the money brought in from the stock issue that has been put into short-term investments until it is needed.

	1994	1995	1996	1997	1998	1999	2000	2001	2002	2003
Revenues	14.0	25.3	26.1	14.7	20.1	29.5	23.1	37.9	57.4	91.1
COGS	7.6	10.6	11.0	4.8	5.0	6.6	7.5	15.7	20.7	27.1
Gross Profit	6.4	14.7	15.1	9.9	15.1	22.9	15.6	22.2	36.7	63.9
Operating Expenses										
SG&A	5.0	8.4	11.6	5.7	7.3	9.1	9.7	13.0	20.7	34.1
R&D	3.5	15.1	3.3	1.0	2.8	3.8	3.6	4.9	5.8	9.5
Other	0.0	0.0	0.0	1.1	1.2	1.2	1.2	1.5	0.9	1.8
Operating Income	(2.1)	(8.8)	0.1	2.1	3.8	8.8	1.1	2.8	9.3	18.4
Interest and Other Income	(0.4)	(1.2)	(0.4)	(0.5)	0.5	0.7	0.6	0.0	0.9	1.9
Earnings Before Taxes	(1.7)	(10.0)	(0.3)	1.6	4.3	9.6	1.7	2.8	10.2	20.4
Taxes	—	0.2	0.1	0.7	1.8	3.6	0.7	1.3	3.5	7.2
Earnings After Taxes	(1.7)	(10.1)	(0.4)	0.8	2.6	6.0	1.0	1.5	6.7	13.2

Figure 9-1. Advanced Neuromodulation Systems, Inc. income statement ($ mil.)

	1994	1995	1996	1997	1998	1999	2000	2001	2002	2003
Cash Flows from Operations	(1.5)	(1.5)	(0.5)	2.5	7.0	2.2	1.9	3.1	7.5	16.5
Cash Flows from Investments	0.3	(14.1)	(3.5)	(5.7)	20.8	0.5	(2.7)	(3.1)	(91.1)	(26.4)
Cash Flows from Financing	0.6	16.9	3.3	3.3	(16.9)	(6.0)	(0.1)	1.0	84.9	7.5
Free Cash Flow	(2.5)	(3.0)	(2.4)	1.2	5.3	(3.7)	0.7	0.0	1.3	(2.4)

Figure 9-2. Advanced Neuromodulation Systems, Inc. cash flow statement ($ mil.)

	1994	1995	1996	1997	1998	1999	2000	2001	2002	2003
Assets										
Current Assets										
Cash	0.1	1.3	0.7	0.8	11.7	8.4	8.6	9.8	11.0	8.5
Short-Term Investments	5.2	2.6	1.4	1.5	0.6	0.4	1.0	2.2	85.8	86.2
Accounts Receivable	1.7	5.0	4.8	2.4	3.1	3.8	3.9	6.5	10.9	18.1
Inventory	4.0	6.1	8.4	3.0	2.6	6.0	5.7	9.8	13.7	22.1
Other Current Assets	0.7	1.7	1.3	15.8	8.2	1.8	2.9	3.3	2.3	3.7
Total Current Assets	11.6	16.7	16.6	23.4	26.2	20.4	22.0	31.5	123.7	138.8
Long-Term Assets										
PP&E	9.6	10.3	11.2	7.4	1.9	5.7	5.3	7.2	10.6	21.1
Intangibles	3.0	17.5	21.2	17.9	17.2	17.2	16.4	16.6	23.5	33.5
Other Long-Term Assets	0.0	0.0	0.0	0.3	0.2	0.3	1.7	0.5	0.6	1.3
Total Assets	24.2	44.5	49.0	49.0	45.5	43.6	45.4	55.9	158.3	194.8

Figure 9-3. Advanced Neuromodulation Systems, Inc. balance sheet (continued on the next page)

	1994	1995	1996	1997	1998	1999	2000	2001	2002	2003
Liabilities and Equity										
Current Liabilities										
Accounts Payable	1.0	1.2	2.3	0.2	0.9	1.8	0.8	1.8	2.4	5.7
Short-Term Debt	2.8	1.6	2.1	8.3	3.6	–	–	0.1	–	–
Taxes Payable	–	–	–	–	2.3	0.5	–	–	0.8	–
Accrued Liabilities	0.5	1.7	1.1	0.8	2.1	1.9	2.1	3.3	5.1	5.4
Other Short-Term Liabilities	0.0	0.0	0.0	0.0	0.9	0.0	0.0	1.4	1.1	1.2
Total Current Liabilities	4.2	4.5	5.5	9.3	9.8	4.2	2.9	6.6	9.4	12.4
Long-Term Liabilities										
Long-Term Debt	4.1	8.6	11.9	3.6	–	–	–	0.1	–	–
Other Long Term Debt	0.0	0.6	0.6	2.2	2.4	2.3	2.3	2.3	3.9	4.3
Total Liabilities	8.3	13.6	18.0	15.1	12.2	6.5	5.2	9.1	13.3	16.7
Total Equity	15.9	30.9	31.0	33.9	33.3	37.0	40.2	46.8	145.0	178.1
Total Liabilities and Equity	24.2	44.5	49.0	49.0	45.5	43.6	45.4	55.9	158.3	194.8

Figure 9-3. Advanced Neuromodulation Systems, Inc. balance sheet (continued)

As you can see already, much information about a company can be gleaned from the three financial statements. Here, we can quickly see that ANS has entered a growth mode and added substantial equity capital to underwrite that growth. They have clearly chosen the financial strategy of funding growth with equity rather than debt, since they have no long-term debt at all.

However, no financial analysis is complete without considering financial ratios and comparing them with both the company's earlier figures and the industry's current figures. Let's look again at the individual financial statements and then consider a few of the more significant financial ratios.

Cash Flow Statement

Despite the importance of the income statement as a financial analysis tool, the success of growing businesses may hinge more on cash flow than on net income. Cash is the lifeblood of a business. A business may show a profit on paper and still not have sufficient cash to operate. Conversely, in some cases, a company may show little or no profit but generate substantial cash each year.

Make sure you give sufficient attention to the cash flow statement. Cash is what you take to the bank. It is what pays the bills.

In our example of Advanced Neuromodulation Systems, we showed the financial statements for each year. For smaller high-growth businesses, it is important to look at monthly income statements and cash flow statements to see how changes occur within a single year. There are three reasons for this.

First, if sales are made on credit, the registering of a sale does not mean that cash is received. The firm may not actually receive the cash for 60 to 90 days. Second, payments for inventory may be required at the time of ordering or receiving products, but the products may not be actually sold for several months. Many businesses have a distinct seasonal effect throughout the year and they go through extreme ebbs and flows of cash. Third, some expenses may be recorded on a uniform monthly basis when payment for the expense is actually either quarterly or annual. Therefore, cash outflows seldom match cash inflows and a business can be cash poor in spite of making money on every sale.

Income Statement

Whereas the cash flow statement measures the movement of cash into and out of the business, the income statement looks at profit and loss. These are not the same. The income statement, for example, takes into account a number of noncash expenses, such as depreciation. The income statement, interestingly, can paint different pictures of the health of a business depending on the way some items are measured. Depreciation can be measured in different ways and inventory can be accounted for in at least two different ways that can impact net income. Important items in the income statement include revenues, cost of goods sold, gross profit margin, selling and administrative expense, interest expense, and taxes.

The importance of looking closely at the income statement is illustrated by the two acronyms EBIT and EBITDA. These refer to *earnings before interest and taxes* and *earnings before interest, taxes, depreciation, and amortization.* In either of these cases, the focus is much more on the operating income or earnings from operations than on earnings after the nonoperational items are considered.

Balance Sheet

The balance sheet is a snapshot of the condition of the company at a point in time, usually the last day of its fiscal year. The balance sheet measures what the company owns (assets), what it owes (liabilities), and what it is worth (equity or net worth). Assets include current assets, such as cash and marketable securities, and fixed assets, such as PP&E minus accumulated depreciation. Note that in the ANS example they are quite heavy in cash and short-term investments. This is because of their stock issue in 2002. Liabilities include both short-term liabilities, such as bank loans, and long-term debt, such as mortgages, bonds, and other long-term liabilities. Equity includes the original equity put in by owners, additions from sales of stock, and additions or subtractions of undistributed profits or losses.

The balance sheet is a snapshot of the condition of the company at a point in time, usually the last day of its fiscal year.

Financial Ratios

Analyzing the three financial statements—balance sheet, income statement, and cash flow statement—provides a wealth of information with which to assess the financial health of a business. Even more information can be obtained by tracking ratios of variables taken from the financial statements. The dozens of ratios that can be computed fall into four categories: *liquidity* ratios, *activity* ratios, *leverage* ratios, and *profitability* ratios. A few ratios from within the four categories can be tracked and computed easily.

Liquidity Ratios

These ratios indicate the firm's capacity for meeting its short-run or near-term cash obligations. In other words, these ratios help in determining whether the business has enough working capital to get by, pay its bills, invest in the future, take advantage of immediate opportunities, and fight off unforeseen short-term crises. The two most important of these are the current ratio and the acid test or quick ratio.

The *current ratio* is derived by dividing current assets by current liabilities. The measure varies considerably from industry to industry. For example, if the industry is one in which the bulk of sales are made on credit, a larger current ratio may be needed for comfort. A business with a high amount of expensive inventory would be expected to have high current assets. The size of the current ratio is also a function of how the inventory and company operations are financed. If short-term debt is used, the ratio will be lower than if long-term debt or equity is used. The desirability of a high ratio also depends on how conservative management is. A very conservative manager may want high inventories, high amounts of cash, and high accounts receivable to feel secure. However, inventory uses up cash that could be used for other purposes and a liberal accounts receivable policy means underwriting customers' debt at no interest. In addition, keeping excess cash or short-term investments on hand may mean that those funds are not being invested to their maximum potential.

It is important to know how a firm compares with its industry and how it compares with itself in previous periods. In the ANS example, note the changes that have occurred in current ratio over the years. Also, note the industry average for the medical equipment industry in 2003. As you will see, the ANS current ratio has been higher than the medical equipment industry for most of the 10-year period. More importantly, note the current ratio for ANS in 2002 and 2003. As you should already expect, the cash and marketable securities jumped significantly when the additional stock issue was completed. Since current liabilities did not jump, the ratio increased dramatically. A jump of this magnitude obviously needs explaining. In this case, the answer is obvious: there is a temporary jump for a period as ANS prepared for growth by issuing new stock. We should expect the current ratio to fall over the next few years as the new equity capital is used for facilities and other growth-related activities.

	2003 Ind Average	1994	1995	1996	1997	1998	1999	2000	2001	2002	2003
C.R.	2.5	2.76	3.7	3.0	2.5	2.7	4.9	7.6	4.8	13.1	11.2
Q.R.	1.7	1.66	1.97	1.26	.50	1.57	2.99	4.62	2.79	11.45	9.10

Figure 9-4. Advanced Neuromodulation Systems, Inc. current and quick ratios, 1994-2003

The *quick ratio* (sometimes called the *acid test ratio*) is computed by subtracting inventory from current assets and dividing the result by current liabilities. Because inventories may not be easily converted to cash, the quick ratio gives a more accurate picture of a firm's capacity for short-run response to opportunities and crises by subtracting the value of these inventories. The quick ratio suggests that ANS is in good short-term financial health. Again, note the effect of the stock offering in 2002.

Efficiency Ratios

These ratios offer insight into how efficiently the firm is using its resources.

The *inventory turnover ratio* is computed by dividing cost of goods sold by average inventory. Again, rules of thumb vary depending on the industry. Therefore, it's valuable to compare the inventory turnover ratio in a business with the industry average as well as with a company's historical ratios. The inventory turnover ratio for Advanced Neuromodulation Systems has ranged from a low of .9 in 1997 to over 2.0 in 1995 and 2001.

	1994	1995	1996	1997	1998	1999	2000	2001	2002	2003
Inventory	1.9	2.1	1.5	0.9	1.8	1.5	1.3	2.0	1.8	1.5
A/R	7.5	7.6	5.3	4.1	7.3	8.5	6.1	7.3	6.6	6.3
Asset	0.6	0.7	0.6	0.3	0.4	0.7	0.5	0.8	0.5	0.5
Fixed Asset	1.5	2.6	2.4	1.6	4.3	7.8	4.2	6.1	6.4	5.7

Figure 9-5. Advanced Neuromodulation Systems, Inc. efficiency ratios, 1994-2003

The *accounts receivable turnover ratio* is computed by dividing annual credit sales by average accounts receivable. Accounts receivable turnover reflects the time it takes to collect credit sales. The ratio should be monitored carefully and compared with industry standards; it is most frequently used to check the receivables collection rate. ANS's receivables have stayed in a healthy range around 7.0, suggesting that they have made good use of the accounts receivables.

The *asset turnover ratio* is computed by dividing sales by total assets. Related to that is the *fixed asset turnover ratio,* which shows the efficiency of the company's fixed assets. ANS's asset turnover ratio has ranged from 0.3 to 0.8 and its fixed asset turnover ratio was a low of 1.5 in 1994 and over 6.4 in 2002. This reflects the growth they were achieving during the last few years and indicates that they were becoming more and more efficient as they grew. At ANS, the fixed asset turnover may be more important, especially in the past two years since the stock issue.

Leverage Ratios

Leverage ratios indicate the extent to which the business's capital is secured through debt rather than equity. These figures are quite critical for a new or growing firm because its ability to raise additional capital may be affected by the present leverage position.

The *debt-to-assets ratio* indicates the percentage of assets that are funded through debt and is measured by dividing total liabilities by total assets. A ratio that is too high may be risky. Too much debt may restrict growth and the ability to raise additional funds externally. Conversely, a low debt-to-assets ratio may indicate inefficient use of invested capital. ANS is, of course, showing a zero long-term *debt-to-equity ratio* since it does not use long-term debt. Its *total-liabilities-to-equity ratio* is also quite low because total liabilities consist of only short-term debt and a small amount of other liabilities.

The *debt-to-equity ratio* indicates the extent to which operating funds have been generated by the owner and is computed by dividing total debt by total owner's equity. Again, this is low for ANS because of their aversion to debt.

An important leverage consideration for many growth-oriented businesses is where to obtain financing for growth.

An important leverage consideration for many growth-oriented businesses is where to obtain financing for growth. ANS funded its growth through the stock offering. However, for many businesses, questions of where and how the business will secure the funds necessary for their growth are not answered as easily, and the answers may spell the difference between success and failure. Rare is the business that generates sufficient capital through revenues to fund the range of needs it will encounter. Therefore, outside sources must be used and two fundamental concerns must be addressed. If the company is highly leveraged, it has limited its additional growth without a substantial infusion of cash, which almost surely must come from equity. Yet, even equity may be difficult to achieve if the company is highly leveraged, because investors may see the leverage as a sign of weakness. Either debt capital or equity capital may be desired, but both may be difficult to achieve.

Recognizing sources of capital is only the first step. It is also necessary to identify and clearly understand the cost of capital. The managers of growth businesses have to decide whether debt or equity costs more. Debt brings the cost of interest and servicing the debt. Equity brings the dilution of ownership and reduced earnings per share unless the earnings increase substantially. Cost of capital is not limited to purely financial terms. Some capital sources impose definite restrictions on the business, affect its flexibility, and alter the managers' degree of control—costs that must be understood and balanced.

Profitability Ratios

Profitability ratios measure a firm's financial performance and financial returns. They are important on their own as they pertain to a particular company and as they compare with industry averages. Significant deviations from industry standards or strong negative movements internally may signal that the economic viability of the business is in serious question. In short, profitability ratios give a quick, bottom-line picture of the firm's current financial results.

Gross profit margin indicates how selling activity provides the margin to cover operating costs and leave a profit balance, a ratio also reported directly on the comparative percentage statements. Returning to the ANS example, the medical equipment industry's average gross profit margin was 63.76 percent in 2003 and its net profit margin was 19.82 percent. Return on investment was 14.62 percent and return on equity was 18.78 percent. How did Advanced Neuromodulation Systems compare? From the income statement, we know that in 2003 ANS had revenues of $91.1 million and a gross profit of $63.9 million. That gives a gross profit margin of 70.1 percent, slightly higher than the industry average. Their operating margin was virtually identical to the industry average of 20 percent, but their net profit margin was 14.5 percent, considerably lower than the industry average of nearly 20 percent.

The *return on total assets ratio* measures a firm's operating performance and is calculated by dividing net income from operations by average total assets. It is the rate of return on the total investment made by creditors and owners. The ANS *return on assets* (ROA) was negative from 1994 through 1996, climbed to over 13 percent in 1998 and 1999, dropped to 2.14 percent in 2000 because of the decreased revenues and resulting profits, and climbed back to 7.49 percent in 2003—still considerably lower than the industry average of 11 percent. The wide variation of ANS's ROA over time and its lower ROA than the industry average suggests a certain amount of risk.

Return on equity (ROE) measures the return just for equity investors. High levels of ROE entice investors to get still more involved financially with the company. Like ROA, ANS showed a negative ROE in 1994 through 1996, with a spike in 1999 and 2000 before the declining revenue and profit brought the ratio down in 2000 and 2001. Substantial growth in revenues and profit in 2002 and especially in 2003 brought the ROE back up 8.18 percent, compared with 18.78 percent for the industry. The issuance of additional stock may have also diluted the ROE figures for 2002 and 2003.

Drawing Strategic Growth Conclusions

Conclusions are often more difficult to draw than financial ratios are to compute. Indeed, in assessing a firm's financial state, ratios and statement comparisons must be used as tools to guide planners in their decisions. The Advanced Neuromodulation Systems example we have used throughout this chapter has illustrated well the changes in the financial health of a company that come from a growth orientation and from infusions of equity capital. You must look carefully at your own company just as we have done here. You must look at changes in the numbers and determine why those changes occur. You must compare them with the industry numbers and with numbers for your own company in prior years. Only when you look dynamically over time and across the industry can you get a really good picture of the ability of your company to compete and grow.

But these measures are only one of the possible information sources that should be considered. Your knowledge and awareness of the business may be necessary, either to temper or to augment what the financial information projects. Good sense and perspective must be used in conjunction with objective figures and computations.

Strategic thinking should pervade the entire financial analysis. For example, a low current ratio suggests that the firm could have trouble paying its bills. However, the strategic significance is that any substantial adverse change in the net use of funds may cause the firm's liquidity position to worsen. Long-term capital may need to be secured to underwrite the strategy and clean up the current liquidity problem.

Similarly, leverage ratios may suggest strong or weak positions in regard to debt versus capital, but they may also dictate a financial strategy before a planned expansion. Interpretations of ratio analyses and financial statement information are the basis for three financial resource evaluations. First, what is the overall financial performance of your business? A number of items may need to be considered in reaching this conclusion. Second, is your company able to raise needed capital? Cash flows, availability of internal funds, and a firm's debt position may all be important considerations. Finally, is your firm's financial condition vulnerable to downturns in revenues or profits? Does it have sufficient resources to bounce back from adversity?

It may appear overly simplistic to reduce the evaluation of financial resources to these three questions, but they are typically the three most critical a business owner must ask before committing to the pursuit of any growth objective, adopting an aggressive strategy, or capturing a new opportunity.

What you have seen here is a guideline for analyzing your financial condition. That financial condition is the baseline. It is the foundation for growth. But like a house consists of more than a foundation alone, a business pursuing growth must have more than just a financial foundation. It must have human resources. It must have production capacity and capabilities. And it must have strengths in marketing if it is going to compete. In the next chapter, we show how to analyze those HR, operational, and marketing resources as they underpin your company's growth strategy.

Note

1.www.ans-medical.com (accessed September 2004).

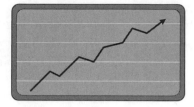

Chapter 10

Can You Get There from Here?

K EVIN TREMBLAY STARTED MIDWEST DIAGNOSTIC MANAGEMENT LLC (MDM) in June 2000. It networks independently owned medical diagnostic radiology centers that provide magnetic resonance imaging (MRI) and computed tomography (CT) scans and streamlines the preferred provider organization (PPO) process for doctors, patients, and insurers. Tremblay thought the company might eventually grow to 20 employees; it is now at 89 in less than five years. The reason for their growth was simply that they provided good customer service to their clients and they received so many inquiries that they had to either grow or get out of the business. They chose to grow.

MDM had revenue of $1.6 million in year one and $34 million in 2004. How did they grow so fast? Tremblay says they were very careful in hiring people to make sure that they were getting the right people. He also makes sure their customers are the right ones for them. They are careful to spend a little extra time working with potential clients to make sure that there is a good fit between MDM and the clients. Even though their growth has been rapid, Tremblay believes in going slow and watching all the details.[1]

When people ask, "Do you have what it takes to grow a business?" they often have in mind the personality of the entrepreneur. Although that is an important factor, it certainly isn't the most important factor leading to success. In fact, many different types of entrepreneurs can be successful. Consider the flamboyant Donald Trump or the in-your-face style of Carly Fiorina of Hewlett-Packard. Contrast those styles with the quieter but equally effective style of Michael Dell. Clearly, there is no one best personality or style for entrepreneurs. What accounts for growth is how well entrepreneurs can marshal the resources necessary to grow a company. Indeed, one of the many definitions of entrepreneurship is the marshalling of resources necessary to capture an opportunity.

We discussed in the last chapter the need to run the numbers, assess the financial health of your company, and determine whether there are sufficient financial resources to underwrite growth. But you need to go further. You need to look at the marketing resources. You need to study your production capabilities. And you need to carefully consider whether you have the right mix of human resources to get the growth you want.

Can you get there from here? As you read this chapter, keep a focus on the strengths and weaknesses of your company. Perhaps keep a check sheet handy to ask yourself if any part of your operation will hold you back. And while you are at it, make note of aspects of the company that will give you a boost to the next level.

Evaluating Marketing Resources

Marketing resources are rarely subjected to close analysis or scrutiny. A business often has no valid measure of the relative effectiveness of its marketing efforts. And because managers often fail to understand the capacity and limitations of their marketing system, they make decisions that lead to failure or waste of resources. But you can do better than that. You *can* get there from here if you analyze your company's marketing efforts carefully to make sure that they can help you achieve the growth you want.

In analyzing the strengths and weaknesses of your marketing system, you should consider eight general categories of marketing resources: market performance, knowledge of markets, location, product, advertising and promotion, price, image, and distribution.

Market Performance

A logical starting point is to evaluate or rate actual market performance. The most reasonable and tangible factor to consider is your company's relative market share. We may occasionally have enough information about the industry, market area, and competitors to calculate an objective and accu-

Marketing resources are rarely subjected to close analysis or scrutiny. A business often has no valid measure of the relative effectiveness of its marketing efforts.

rate statement of market share. More often, we can develop only an estimate of market share based on sketchy or piecemeal data. This is especially true in new businesses or businesses in the early stages of growth whose managers do not have a good sense of the market. This can also be difficult when competing in an industry made of mostly privately held companies for which determining sales or market share is extremely difficult.

Market share is one indicator of a company's performance that addresses past performance. Even though it indicates little about future potential, useful inferences may be drawn from it. For example, if the market is becoming saturated and prospects for industry growth are limited, the strength or weakness of present market share is probably a key indicator of whether the business will be able to withstand and survive an industry shakeout. On the other hand, if the industry segment is new or undergoing substantial growth, market share is difficult to assess. But it also may be the least important consideration. If the market is growing rapidly, the most important issue may be your company's ability to compete and grow rather than capture market share.

Market share is one indicator of a company's performance that addresses past performance. Even though it indicates little about future potential, useful inferences may be drawn from it.

So what do we conclude about market performance? You must do whatever you can to understand your relative position, but your stage in the industry life cycle will determine how concerned you need to be about that position.

Knowledge of Markets

When considering your overall market performance, you must consider what you know about the market. For example, you must first know and understand your target markets. Who are your customers? What is the demographic makeup of the target market and how is it changing? Perhaps most important, what are customer preferences and needs and how will these be changing in the future? You must also know your geographical market area. What changes or developments are occurring that may affect the business? Is the demographic composition of the market area changing? Are important new competitors entering the market area? You must be aware of important market changes and directions. True, knowledge and awareness are intangible concepts and are susceptible to a wide range of interpretations. Yet this knowledge may be most critical in helping position a business to deal with future obstacles and opportunities.

If you are keeping a checklist as we suggested at the beginning of this chapter, write "target market" as a category. Then under it, list as many identifying factors of your target market and how people in that target market think. How large is the market? Is it growing or stable? Are the customers baby boomers, millennials, or something between? Are you dealing with well people or those who are ill? Is the end user the actual purchaser or a decision maker regarding the product or service? Are you likely to have repeat buyers or is the product a one-time purchase, such as a wheelchair? Add any other descriptors of your market. Then ask yourself how certain you are about your answers. Even a best guess can be refined later.

> A target market is that group of customers who account for most of your revenue. It may be defined in terms of demographics, location, types of customers, or even uses of the product. You may want to break down the target market further by having a primary target market that accounts for half your sales and a secondary market that accounts for another 25 percent, with all others making up the remaining 25 percent.

Location

Location may or may not be relevant for your business. But it can also be a factor in your growth strategy. If you face a national market that is easily serviced by distributors, location may not be important from a customer standpoint. If your market is primarily regional or requires personal service, locating a business near customers becomes more important.

Control is a key factor related to location. For example, Culver's is a rapidly growing chain of upscale fast food featuring frozen custard and ButterBurgers®. It was started in 1984 in Wisconsin by Craig Culver and now has more than 200 restaurants in 15 states. When Culver decided to franchise and enter a growth mode, he consciously made the decision to allow franchises only within a day's drive of their headquarters. He consciously expanded in the near geographical area in order to be able to control operations better. He is now expanding the geographical area into additional states as the demand for the high-quality fast food attracts more and more potential franchisees.

We include two tables that may be of interest to you as you look for growth locations. These assume that you are searching for additional locations. The first chart is for retail businesses and the second is for manufacturing firms. Use these charts as a starting point and then add to them as necessary. Consider these factors for the business in general. That is, develop the factors before you select locations. This keeps you from rationalizing a good or bad decision based on one or two items about locations you already know about. You should have several factors listed. You may even want to rank the factors in terms of importance to the business. Once you have listed important factors, then rate possible locations on each of the factors, as excellent, good, fair, or poor. With this ranking and rating system, you should be able to get a rough idea of the best locations for the business. You can then proceed to negotiate terms with the owners of the property.

Factor	Excellent	Good	Fair	Poor
General location in city or region				
Proximity to primary target market				
Proximity to competitors				
Demographics of target market				
Size of building and lot				
Traffic count at the location				
Speed of traffic passing the location				
Distance from traffic signal or stop sign				
Visibility				

Figure 10-1. Location factors for retail businesses

Factor	Excellent	Good	Fair	Poor
General region of country				
Proximity to transportation				
Types of available transportation				
Condition of available structures				
Inducements from city				
Availability of labor				
Strength of unions in community				
Tax rates				

Figure 10-2. Location factors for manufacturing businesses

For some businesses, such as those providing services, in which the business representative goes to customers' homes or offices, the specific location may be immaterial.

Product

As you plan for growth, you must evaluate the appeal of the products sold. Although products can be evaluated in absolute terms, the rating should also reflect the relative strength of the products from a competitive perspective. Three product-related aspects should be considered: the product line, the quality of the product, and the service provided with the product.

The *product line* refers to the variety of products your company offers. You must consider both the breadth and the depth of the product line. A broad or complete line enables the business to meet a wide range of consumer needs; depth refers to the choices available within a product category. For example, one shoe store may offer a very narrow product line, limiting its business exclusively to shoes but offering a great number of styles and sizes. A competing store, presenting a broader product line, offers not only shoes but also an array of complementary or supportive products, such as polishes, socks, purses, and leather goods. Frequently, the store with the narrow line can still compete because of the depth of styles and sizes. The evaluation of the product line must consider not only competitive influences but also the strategic approach the business is trying to promote. If you visualize the company as a specialty business, for example, your product line should reflect this strategy.

A second product-related decision relates to the *quality* of the company's products. Here, you need to view both product image and product quality from a consumer or market perspective. Purchases are made on the basis of perceived image and quality. As you plan for growth, you must determine precisely what level of quality and image you want to promote. Indeed, the decision about product quality is strategic rather than just operational. The quality of your products defines the company in the eyes of customers. In retail, consider Nordstrom or Neiman Marcus versus Kmart or Wal-Mart. One may not be any more profitable than the other, but every decision the company makes is based on the quality projected. Similarly, in automobile manufacturing, Ford owns Jaguar and Volvo in addition to its traditional line of cars. Certainly quality is important throughout the company, but quality is the overall focus in Jaguar while a Ford Focus is produced with price-sensitive customers in mind. You should strive to obtain an objective and unbiased evaluation of these factors. Determine what quality and image you intend to project and then measure how well you project that image.

Finally, you must consider product *service*, which relates to the firm's assurances that it will address consumer concerns about products effective-

Although products can be evaluated in absolute terms, the rating should also reflect the relative strength of the products from a competitive perspective.

ly and fully after the sale. Product warranties are important, as are the number, availability, and quality of service representatives and service technicians. You may be well aware of some companies—Caterpillar, for example—that are as well known for service as they are for their products.

Can you measure service? Certainly. Measure customer satisfaction. Measure complaints. Look at ratings by outside organizations. Can service become a competitive weapon as you plan for growth? Absolutely.

Promotion

The promotion mix for a company consists of its personal selling, advertising, publicity, and sales promotion.

The promotion mix for a company consists of its personal selling, advertising, publicity, and sales promotion. You need to evaluate the strength of your promotion efforts. You should gather as much objective evidence of the effectiveness of these efforts as possible. In some cases, this is readily available. For example, a business may note sales growth following certain advertising campaigns. Often, however, such information is not available, making promotion one of the most difficult areas to assess. You realize, of course, the significance of reaching consumers, informing them of your company's products, and encouraging them to make purchases. Overall advertising and other promotional emphases, however, are hard to analyze from an objective and competitive perspective. This is one reason why managers often feel that advertising and promotion is one of the most expendable resources. The promotion budget is one of the first to be reduced or eliminated when the small business encounters financial strains. Ironically, this is often precisely the wrong strategic decision.

To evaluate the firm's promotion activities, you must have a feel for how important these factors are to the industry in which the business operates. If competitors in the industry rely heavily on advertising to generate sales, for example, then meager and ineffective advertising and promotion may be a significant weakness. However, if industry sales are driven by a few established and regular customers, large investments in advertising and promotion may be unnecessary. It may be useful to compare your expenditures for advertising and promotion with those typical of the industry and with those of immediate competitors. If competitors are investing heavily in advertising, a similar response may be necessary to keep or gain market share. Trade associations are helpful in determining industry trends or norms with which a company's promotional efforts may be compared.

In some industries, personal selling is the key to success. This is especially true in business-to-business selling and in some service businesses. Even in retail businesses, the sales force must be analyzed. Personal selling can be studied by looking at sales per salesperson, sales per department, or sales per product line.

Keys to Personal Selling

Establish rapport.
Know your product.
Know competing products and their weaknesses.
Provide immediate responses to questions.
Deliver what you promise.

Even publicity can be studied. A company can get free publicity in a number of ways—working for charitable causes that might do a press release noting contributions, sending news items to local newspapers, offering to be interviewed as "experts" in a human interest broadcast on television, and holding contests for prizes. Such efforts should not be done randomly but should be carefully planned to get the most return for the effort.

Price

Price should reflect the strategy or image the business wants to project. Price is certainly cost-based. But price also sends a message to customers about the quality and image of your company and its products. A discount store, for example, makes a statement with its low prices, but managers stressing quality, service, or exclusivity often set prices higher to reflect a higher image.

Price is certainly cost-based. But price also sends a message to customers about the quality and image of your company and its products.

The strength or weakness of a pricing strategy is strongly influenced by the competition. An owner may set prices based on costs (for raw materials, assembly, sales expenses, and others) and be unable to lower them to realize an acceptable return. But if a key competitor lowers its prices, the company's inability to respond accordingly may be viewed as a price weakness. On the other hand, price may be rated a definite strength when size of operations, economies of scale, and production efficiency enable a business to offer products at consistently lower prices than the competition.

Image

Image has both internal and external ramifications. The image of the business is reflected through its internal culture or climate and in that way affects the employees. In addition, the image is perceived by those outside the business and affects their attitudes toward the business. The image should be consistent with the strategies of the business, in which case image emerges as an important strength. Otherwise, image can be a weakness. If a business wishes to stress personal service as a competitive factor, for example, it should present an image reflecting openness, concern for workers, communication, and trust. If quality is being stressed, an image of high skill, training, and attention to detail is valuable.

Image evolves as the firm continues in operation. The public's perception of the image is based on historical exposure to the firm. If you have purchased a business, mistakes made by previous owners may affect the image of your business. If this is the case, you need to recognize image as a problem area and work to change the public's perception. Because changes tend to be incremental, remember that image definitely affects customer attitudes toward the business and, in turn, the consumption pattern of customers.

Image is, unfortunately, difficult to measure accurately, but you can get a good feel for it through such informal measures as complaints (or lack of complaints), word of mouth, and recommendations from satisfied customers.

Image is, unfortunately, difficult to measure accurately, but you can get a good feel for it through such informal measures as complaints (or lack of complaints), word of mouth, and recommendations from satisfied customers. In addition, surveys of name or brand awareness and factors related to image can provide very useful information if done well. No matter what image is sought, you must work to present a consistent image that is carefully planned and developed.

Distribution

Are the channels of distribution accessible and acceptable? Does the product flow from the business to customers in a reasonable and cost-effective way? In many cases, your product reaches the ultimate consumer only after passing through intermediaries. If you are a manufacturer, you may distribute directly to retailers or to a wholesaler, who in turn sells to retailers or to both retailers and wholesalers. You may need to evaluate each stage of the distribution process to gain a clear notion of the relative strength of the entire system.

Analyzing distribution for a manufacturing firm should consider everything from the point at which the product comes off the assembly line to the point when the final user receives the product. This may include warehousing, inventory policies, shipping methods, and billing.

Two factors are important in analyzing distribution: cost and coverage. The two factors tend to work against each other. A manufacturing firm, for example, may find that it is cheaper to distribute products directly to customers, but it can reach only a few customers. By using intermediaries such as wholesalers and retailers, it incurs added cost but it can achieve significant increases in market coverage. Often in these cases, the cost of the intermediaries is far outweighed by the increase in coverage.

Few measures are available to indicate that distribution is being done well, but there are indications that it is being done poorly. Products sitting in the loading dock area for an excessive length of time, for example, indicate poor distribution. Stockouts among retail stores, even though the manufacturing plant is not overworked, are another indication of problems with distribution. And if the cost of distribution seems out of line, the area needs to be studied.

Evaluating Operational Resources

Operational resources are those that are involved with or that support the production of a product or service. They may relate to the physical elements of a job or to relationships within the business and with key contacts outside the business. Clearly, relevant resources are numerous, but five key areas must be evaluated: production facilities, access to suppliers, inventory control, organization structure, and quality control.

Production Facilities

In looking at your production capabilities, the first step is to evaluate the firm's plant and equipment. Is the physical plant large enough to handle the desired growth in your business operations? Have you made the technical advances in plant and equipment necessary to remain competitive? Is your equipment technically and operationally sound and efficient?

In looking at your production capabilities, the first step is to evaluate the firm's plant and equipment.

Part of this analysis should address the issue of capacity. Are you operating near capacity or significantly below capacity? If you are planning for growth, the capacity can be a major weakness. It is critical that you assess this carefully. Suppose, for example, that you think the market will allow you to capture a 25 percent growth over the next year. If you are near capacity, how will you produce the products for that level of growth? Can you outsource that much of the production? Can you find excess capacity in another location of your business? Is there idle capacity in the area that you can lease and adapt to your needs?

Recall our discussion of Advanced Neuromodulation Systems in the previous chapter. In 2002, ANS made a major stock offering. Part of those funds were used to acquire distributors of their products. A significant part, however, was to increase production capacity for their growing market.

They realized that they did not have the capability to grow at the rate they desired and they used equity capital to develop their capacity.

Access to Suppliers

A promising opportunity may be hurt by either costly or inconsistent sources of supply.

Two basic questions emerge here. The first concerns basic availability. Do you have ready access to necessary raw materials and suppliers? The second question concerns the cost considerations that must temper availability. How much do materials and supplies cost? A promising opportunity may be hurt by either costly or inconsistent sources of supply.

You should determine whether to purchase inventory or components from a single supplier or a number of suppliers. This problem is made worse if the industry as a whole is also rapidly growing. This causes availability of components to be a continuing problem. Some manufacturers rely on strategic alliances with suppliers to ensure the availability of quality products. Other manufacturers may go a step further and actually buy their suppliers in order to control the availability of products.

Manufacturers are not the only kind of business to rely on long-term relationships. Retailers have an especially close dependence on suppliers. You must consider that relationship carefully, because customers depend on the retailer to purchase specific brands of products. Changing brand selection or suppliers may adversely affect customer relations. Service businesses typically are not as tied to suppliers as are retailers or manufacturers, but managers of service businesses should still look at the relationship with suppliers as part of an overall internal analysis.

Inventory Control

In examining inventory, you evaluate the strength of your system for stocking, ordering, and reordering materials (raw or finished products). Success in this area may be the key to meeting customers' needs on time. Do you know what materials are on hand at any given time? Can they be located and accessed? Are there clear, established procedures for initiating reorders? Is there usually an acceptable level of materials in stock or is the business regularly plagued with inventory backlogs and outages? As your business grows, the inventory control system may need to become automated. The automation could range from a simple spreadsheet-type program to a completely automated bar-coding system and extra-net that electronically places an order with suppliers' computer-based ordering systems when inventory reaches a certain level.

Growth businesses face an inventory dilemma. Needed inventory must be on hand so that production runs are not hampered and customers are not frustrated at production delays, but inventory-holding costs can be quite formidable. Therefore, if your business plans growth, but you are not sure how fast or how much, you may want to limit inventory to the basic level needed to maintain a consistent flow of operations. This is an option provided by the popular just-in-time (JIT) inventory system. Under the JIT system, the supplier delivers components when, where, and in the quantities needed. Of course, a JIT system is only as effective as the relationship and communication that exists between the business and its suppliers. Automated information systems are essential, so all of the factors discussed here may need to be weighed when evaluating the system of inventory control.

The need for inventory control goes far beyond simply counting inventory. In a high-growth market, you may decide to produce components yourself rather than risk unreliable suppliers. On the other hand, managing substantial amounts of inventory is expensive in addition to the internal cost of producing the products in-house. Growth businesses are often well advised to outsource everything possible to reduce the fixed cost of plant and equipment necessary to produce components in-house.

Organization Structure

The structure of an organization is the formal flow of information and authority within it, indicating the jobs that people do and accompanying areas of responsibility. The organizational structure should be consistent with and support the strategies and objectives of the business. If you want operational flexibility, an informal or open structural system may be preferable. The key to evaluating the structure is to note if the business and its personnel are unduly restricted by the demands of the structure or if the structure is logical and helps employees fulfill their responsibilities.

Managers of growing firms will often choose to structure the business around functional areas, that is, marketing, finance, accounting, human resources, and operations. Others may want to build the structure around particular products. Still others, especially service businesses, may want to structure around particular key customers. The important part of this analysis is to determine whether the structure is as efficient as possible while still allowing the company to achieve its objectives.

A problem that is unique to growth-oriented businesses is the need to change or adjust the structure to accommodate the growth of the business.

The key to evaluating the structure is to note if the business and its personnel are unduly restricted by the demands of the structure or if the structure is logical and helps employees fulfill their responsibilities.

109

Indicators of inefficiencies in structure are miscommunication, delays in getting authority to implement new ideas, problems in dealing with customers, employee complaints, and defects in products. If the problems are indeed caused by an inappropriate structure, solutions may include restructuring around key customers, key products, or key processes to become more attentive to priority areas in the business.

Quality Control

We discussed in earlier sections the importance of determining the appropriate quality strategy for a business and then the necessity to ensure achieving the level of quality desired. Managers of any business must evaluate the policies and procedures that the organization uses to ensure the quality of its products and services. We live in an era when business is held to ever-rising quality standards. In fact, quality is one of the strongest explanations for the long-term success of a business in today's competitive environment. The assessment of quality is important for growing businesses because growth businesses are especially vulnerable during the growth phase. Because the demands of growth will distract your attention, quality may slip. Or you may pay adequate attention to quality, but it may simply be difficult to maintain quality when production lines are operating at full capacity. New, less trained employees hired to help achieve growth may make errors in quality. Running machines at full capacity may lead to breakdowns or inadequate tolerances. Thus, special efforts must be made to assess quality and ensure that it receives adequate emphasis.

The assessment of quality is important for growing businesses because growth businesses are especially vulnerable during the growth phase.

Although quality may be assessed from many perspectives, users of a company's goods and services often offer the most important signals. Customers and clients provide excellent evidence of their satisfaction with quality by their reactions to the products and services they receive. For example, if your business provides components for a large industrial manufacturer, quality specifications are normally stipulated contractually. Failure to meet these standards may mean losing the contract. On the other hand, if your business serves a retail or service market, customer complaints or product returns may signal quality deficiencies.

You should not assume that quality is acceptable simply because customer complaints are not being heard—unacceptable quality may be reflected in decreased sales. A slip in quality is often difficult to detect, and quality comparisons between competitors are often quite subjective and subtle. Therefore, specific procedures must be enacted to detect quality concerns.

Some businesses, for example, rely on customer surveys, whereas others conduct regular internal audits. Whatever set of procedures is used, quality assessment is a critical factor in internal analysis.

Evaluating Human Resources

The final category of internal factors that should be analyzed is your company's human resources. Although this component is often overlooked, a company's employees are among its most critical assets. We view human resources broadly to include all employees and their unique skills and abilities.

An initial concern for growing businesses is to examine the number of employees required and the relevancy of their skills.

An initial concern for growing businesses is to examine the number of employees required and the relevancy of their skills. An owner may be tempted to either overstaff or understaff a growing business either because of grandiose plans or a too limited vision of the firm's potential. You must determine how many employees are needed and what specific skills are required to achieve the desired growth. If required skills are missing, you must either train current employees or hire additional workers with the necessary skills.

As the business grows, human resource planning can become quite complex. This is especially true for companies that are growing rapidly; you often can't hire new employees fast enough to support the growth. It is tempting to want to hire each new employee personally, but that is a time-consuming process. You will soon realize that the recruiting and hiring process has to be delegated to others.

A second human resource consideration is the assessment of employee morale and management-labor relations. In many situations, you need not take the time and effort to conduct a formal morale survey; a set of more informal indicators may suffice. Employee turnover, absenteeism, tardiness, and a general assessment of the work climate should provide a notion of morale. Frequent grumblings, complaints, arguments, and conflicts may indicate weakened morale. Again, you should attempt to ascertain a general feeling about morale as it affects business action. Morale should never be ignored—poorly motivated and uncommitted workers can undermine a well-focused growth strategy.

Although morale is important in any business, it is especially important in a business that is embarking on a concerted growth strategy where the morale and cohesiveness of employees can be critical. In these situations you will depend heavily on employees to carry their share of the load and more.

Often, long hours are required to keep the business going. Employees with good morale are usually willing to put in that extra effort. But if morale is poor, employees are unwilling to put out extra effort and may even have to be cajoled into working at a productive level. Poor morale certainly can slow down the work process and can sometimes be severe enough that a growth strategy may have to be abandoned completely.

A third factor to examine is the business's compensation system—that is, wages and salaries plus any fringe benefits. For our purposes, the essential determinations are whether the present compensation system is both adequate and consistent with the strategic direction of the firm.

The adequacy of compensation is determined by both internal and external comparisons. Internally, most workers will feel compensation is adequate if it is distributed equitably; that is, better performers earn more than lesser performers. However, if considerable work is being done in teams, team members must feel their compensation is fair in relation to one another. Indeed, a perception of equitable compensation is the key to employee motivation and the credibility of the compensation system.

Internally, most workers will feel compensation is adequate if it is distributed equitably; that is, better performers earn more than lesser performers.

From an external perspective, adequacy of compensation is largely a function of competition. Are workers receiving compensation that is reasonably consistent with that of workers in similar firms and industries? Workers may be willing to accept a lower salary if other factors make up for it. Suppose, for example, that two businesses are competing in the same labor market. One provides a slightly higher compensation package, but the second offers a more challenging, interesting, and pleasant work environment.

How to Have Happy Employees

Be careful whom you hire.
Train them well.
Pay them adequately.
Give them challenges that use their brains.
Give them the freedom to make mistakes.

Some workers may feel that the opportunities available at the second business outweigh the compensation difference. But you should not deceive yourself. In general, workers expect compensation that is similar to, or better than, what they could receive elsewhere.

The compensation system must also be consistent with the strategic thrust of the firm. If the firm is moving aggressively into new markets and depending on the efforts of its sales force to attract new customers, the compensation system must reflect this dependence. Quotas, bonuses, or a commission system may be needed to motivate workers to attract new contacts and businesses. Stock options or profit-sharing plans are often used in growth-oriented businesses to motivate employees to strive toward growth.

When compensation is discussed, it is usual to assume that the focus is on dollars. Yet much compensation is not monetary. Such things as office furnishings, company cars, vacation scheduling, and more interpersonal issues can also affect the motivation of employees. For example, your willingness to allow employees to adjust their working hours may have an impact on motivation. If you are attempting to build a unified, loyal workforce with a strong commitment to the business, then companywide performance incentives may be appropriate. A properly designed system can help you achieve your objectives.

A final human resource area that should be assessed is training. Here the question to be answered is whether employees are receiving the training necessary to do their jobs well. Training can be either in-house or off-site. It can be either technical training on how to use new software programs or classes on team building. Training should be ongoing as long as it does not unduly interrupt the actual work of the business. You should have an eye open for indications of the need for training.

One area in which training is important in today's businesses is technology. Computers and software change so rapidly that it's difficult to keep up with developments. Sometimes sending people to half-day or full-day workshops yields productivity far in excess of attempts to train employees in new processes during normal workdays.

In summary, you need to ask yourself three questions. Do I have the right number of employees? Do they have the required skills? Do I have the commitment of the employees to achieve growth?

So, Can You Get There from Here?

Our list of areas or factors to be analyzed is by no means all-inclusive; it is intended to provide a framework for strategic growth planning. Make no mistake: analyzing your strengths and weaknesses is a detailed process and may take considerable amounts of time over several weeks. Quite often, managers from small businesses to *Fortune* 100 companies attempt to perform comprehensive internal analyses by simply attending a half-day retreat to "brainstorm." While this approach may provide creative insights into

In summary, you need to ask yourself three questions. Do I have the right number of employees? Do they have the required skills? Do I have the commitment of the employees to achieve growth?

sources of strengths and weaknesses, when used alone it may also expose a firm to unnecessary risks. When you simply brainstorm to analyze your internal operations, you may overlook critical sources of competitive strengths or weaknesses. Using our framework during a company analysis will decrease the possibility of getting blindsided by missing a source of critical strength or weakness.

Note

1. Nichole L. Torres, "Midwest Diagnostic Management LLC," *Entrepreneur Magazine*, June 2004, p. 76.

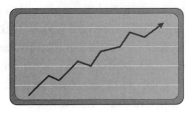

Chapter 11

Yesss!! We're Better Than They Are!

W ILLIAM STONE IS THE FOUNDER, CHAIRMAN OF THE BOARD, CEO, and president of SS&C Technologies, Inc., a provider of enterprise applications software serving the institutional investments industry. SS&C began in 1986 and went public in 1996. It has grown to a company of over 400 people with offices in Europe, Asia, and North America. In a recent interview in *The Wall Street Transcript*, Stone talked about his company, its products, and its competition.[1]

Stone noted that their market is broad with a lot of players. They have strong competitors in each of their market segments. But he feels they have some real competitive advantages in their broad range of products, allowing customers to do one-stop shopping. In addition, they sell in multiple venues, giving them a broader range of selling capability than their competitors. Other strengths of SS&C, according to Stone, are its solid, committed management team, its performance-tied compensation system, the freedom employees have, and the company's drive to succeed.

SS&C's capabilities to continue its growth seem good. They recently did a secondary stock offering that raised $75 million, giving them $116 million in liquid assets on their balance sheet. Yet, Stone would like to see SS&C grow even more. He feels that their recent revenues of $100 million still leave them relatively small. They have made 14 acquisitions over the past 10 years, but are still looking for other businesses to acquire. It appears that SS&C has looked carefully at its competitive markets, has studied its internal capabilities, and is poised to continue growth.

So, you have now read three chapters about the world around you, your competitors, and your customers and their demographics. And you have finished reading three more chapters about how to take a hard look at yourself to see what strengths you have and what weaknesses need to be overcome. You have looked at your financials, your marketing capabilities, your human resources, and your production capacity. Now it is time to put these two sets of information together.

You have looked at your financials, your marketing capabilities, your human resources, and your production capacity. Now it is time to put these two sets of information together.

In particular, you want to look to see how your strengths match the opportunities out there. You want to see how you stack up against your competitors and their strategies. You want to see what opportunities you can exploit because you are better than your competitors. Let's go back to the outside one more time and look at the company's business environment.

Apparent Opportunities and Real Opportunities

When you looked at your business environment, you likely saw a number of possible areas of opportunity. Perhaps competitors had become so big they no longer provided the personal touch that consumers had come to desire and expect. Perhaps new segments or niches in the market were appearing but had not been targeted. Perhaps consumer needs and preferences shifted so that adding complementary products or services would significantly increase sales and profits.

Merely identifying those opportunities, however, does not mean that your company either can or should take advantage of them. You can decide this only after you have taken that hard look at yourself. Consider the following example dealing with a small company in one community.

Changing demographic and social factors within the community suggested that a dinner theater was an attractive opportunity. There was no dinner theater in the community and the increasing population base of young, upscale consumers seemed likely to support one. A particular restaurant in the community accurately recognized this as an environmental opportunity. But their hard look inside clearly revealed that the restaurant had neither the employees nor the financial resources to commit to such a project. Expanding into the dinner theater market would have taken considerable capital, extensive planning, a bigger building, and additional staff who would be willing to play the double role of actors and waiters. In short, the apparent opportunity was not a real opportunity. Apparent opportunities become real business opportunities only when an internal analysis reveals that a business is able to capitalize on these opportunities.

The distinction between apparent opportunities and real business opportunities is critical for growing businesses. Care must be taken to make sure the growth opportunities are the best areas of growth that the business should pursue. This can occur only through a thorough understanding of the company's internal condition. Successful growth requires a careful mesh between opportunities and capacities. Indeed, one of the most insightful responses owners and managers of growing ventures may make is to back away from some apparent opportunities. In some cases, pursuing opportunities—even seemingly promising opportunities—may drain resources to the point that the business is simply spread too thin.

If it looks like a duck and quacks like a duck, it must be a duck. But if it looks like an opportunity, it may not be all it's quacked up to be. You have to study it, analyze it, and determine if it is really an opportunity or just a big idea.

You may be able to identify a number of opportunities. In general, the more dynamic and growth-oriented an industry, the greater the number of opportunities. Similarly, the more open, responsive, and financially sound your business, the greater the number of real business opportunities you are likely to realize.

The distinction between apparent opportunities and real business opportunities may seem somewhat arbitrary or subjective, yet it is critical to strategic planning. You must be concerned with acting only on those opportunities that have survived the scrutiny of internal analysis and become real business opportunities.

The Role of Distinctive Competencies

A distinctive competence is any area, factor, or consideration that gives a business a meaningful competitive edge. Distinctive competencies—activities that your firm does not only well but better than competitors—positively distinguish it from your competitors. Distinctive competencies may include superior products, brand loyalty, great distribution, or technological know-how. They may even include processes used by a firm, such as ISO 9000 certification or an effective just-in-time inventory control system. It may be a patented product that has several years of monopoly protection left.

Distinctive competencies often emerge and grow as you position your company to enhance its competitive position. Consider the case of

117

Amazon.com. You may be surprised to know that Amazon.com started only in 1995. In only 10 years, it has become a huge business. Along the way, it has carefully crafted a distinctive competence: it has found a unique niche in a highly competitive industry by capitalizing on available technology and consumers' growing need for convenience.

> ## Facts about Amazon.com
>
> **Their vision:** To build a place where people can find and discover anything they want online.
> **Number of customers:** 41 million
> **Number of vendors:** 700,000
> **Increase in sales during last year:** 37 percent
> **Categories of products:** Books, music, videos, video games, electronics, toys and baby, tools and hardware, kitchen and housewares, apparel, sports and outdoors, gourmet food, jewelry and watches, health and personal, beauty.

Identifying and Developing Areas of Distinctive Competence

You should investigate areas where you can create a meaningful competence, realizing that the competitive environment, your company's internal capacities, and its reactions within its competitive environment dictate competencies.

Distinctive competencies may appear in either of two ways. One way is their development as part of your company's current operations. Over time, the business operates in such a manner that clear and important competencies are present, perhaps having initially arisen out of the firm's mission or managerial orientation. Over time, they become an integral part of the business.

In some situations, however, distinctive competencies may need to be developed or nurtured—particularly if none currently exist—as is the case with businesses at the beginning of the growth phase. You should analyze the competitive environment, scrutinize internal resources, and carefully and objectively decide which areas are most fruitful for development.

Such a building or development process can be quite trying if you want to grow your company rapidly. Essentially, you should investigate areas where you can create a meaningful competence, realizing that the competitive environment, your company's internal capacities, and its reactions within its competitive environment dictate competencies. Consider the case of cybercafes, for example, that purposefully identify an area of competitive uniqueness and commit energy and resources to develop it. This area becomes a distinctive competence because it meets the needs of today's fast-paced, connected society.

There is not an exhaustive set of competencies that make one company stand out from the rest. However, there are ten typical sources of distinctive competence likely to be recognized by growth-oriented businesses.

Sources of Distinctive Competencies

Quality
Service
Location
Filling a special niche
Protected product
Flexibility and adaptability
Strong consumer orientation
Human resources
Pricing
Technology

Quality is a key area of competence and one that is of growing importance to consumers. Here, a business offers consumers a product or service that is of discernibly higher quality than offered by the competition. Accordingly, consumers come to associate a quality image with the business. Consider the case of Winspec, which we discussed in Chapter 8. At Winspec, quality was defined as virtually zero defects, thereby assuring customers that rework should not be a consideration. That brought down customers' total cost of production. Remember: customers will pay a premium to get better quality.

Service often moves hand in hand with quality. It's a business's efforts to aid consumers in dealing with the business and its products. The efforts to provide service may occur before a sale or when repairs and follow-up are needed after a sale. Service extends beyond the auto mechanic or small specialty business. Lands' End, now owned by Sears, grew based on a strategy of providing good-quality clothes with an absolute return policy. Buy a shirt or slacks or sweater through Lands' End and rest assured that even if it was a special order, they will still take it back—no questions asked. This is exceptional service for a direct mail company.

Location is a factor that often dictates a company's success and can be an area of considerable competence when recognized and exploited. Location may affect a firm's visibility, its likelihood of attracting the target market, and its competitive edge over businesses offering similar products or services.

Filling a special niche is a particularly important competence and one that can be developed after careful analysis of the competitive situation. A business may choose to enter an untapped market, provide unique services or products

Quality is a key area of competence and one that is of growing importance to consumers.

119

(and thus limit direct competition), or add aspects of novelty or originality to existing products. Such extensions and variations must be focused on real needs of some segment of the market, however. Providing a unique product that no one cares about or wants to purchase is counterproductive.

A distinctive competence that can last for many years if exploited appropriately is a *protected product*. You may not have heard of the pharmaceutical company G.D. Searle. But you certainly have encountered its most notable product—aspartame, better known as NutraSweet®. The reason G.D. Searle has done well over the years is that it held a patent on aspartame. Thus, it had a distinctive competence for many years, through acquisition by Monsanto in 1985 and a spinoff as NutraSweet Company, until the patent finally expired in December 1992.

Patents, Copyrights, and Trademarks

Patents last for 20 years from date of filing.

Copyrights last for 70 years after the death of the author or 95 years if the copyright is owned by a company.

Trademarks can last forever if the company continues to use and protect them.

Flexibility and adaptability may be particular strengths your business can focus on that offer a competitive edge over more formalized and more rigid operations. For example, your business may do custom work and thereby attract customers from larger firms that don't offer custom services.

A *strong consumer orientation* is often promoted by growth-oriented companies that are able to stay in closer touch with shifting consumer needs and demands and respond more quickly to them. Consumers are likely to feel that a company's employees know them and are willing to adapt and modify their methods and operations to accommodate customers' individuality.

Human resources can be an area of competence when managers and other employees have extensive experience or knowledge, factors that are business strengths. When customers recognize these strengths and believe they are superior, a distinctive competence exists.

For example, two large grocery stores both have experienced, knowledgeable workers. One store, however, is primarily self-service: customers place their groceries on the checkout conveyor and then sack them after paying. The second store emphasizes personal interaction and help: employees sack the groceries and carry them to the customers' cars. Both stores possess employee-related strengths, but only the second has transferred that strength into a distinctive competency.

Pricing is a tenuous competency—powerful yet remarkably fragile. Technically, it is not price, but cost that is the distinctive competency. The ability to keep costs extremely low leads to possibly the lowest price in the industry. As long as it can keep its cost structure lower than competitors, a company can have a significant share of the market. The potential of pricing as a competency may be significant if competitors are unable to reduce their own costs enough to make their prices competitive. However, if a competitor is willing and able to alter its cost structure, this competency can be stripped of its value very quickly. Price is therefore often viewed as a rather tenuous competency, subject to inroads from aggressive competitors.

Finally, *technology* can be a distinctive competency. The case of Amazon.com, discussed earlier, is a good example of technology as a competency. Their ability to create a web-based market for books, music, and now a variety of products gave them a distinctive competency that has withstood the test of time.

These ten areas are competencies only if a company's customers perceive them as such. Perception is often more important than reality. You may correctly feel that your company's customer service is superior to that of the immediate competition, but service is not a distinctive competency if customers don't perceive it to be. If customers do not recognize that the service is indeed better than provided by competitors, the service is at best an unexploited strength. Effectively marketing a strength is the bridge to creating a distinctive competency.

Effectively marketing a strength is the bridge to creating a distinctive competency.

Let's consider the concept of brand equity. Brand equity is the value associated with your product over competing produces. Some companies have substantial brand equity: their logos or products are instantly recognized by customers and they convey a specific image for that company's products. For example, you instantly get an image of a no-frills, well-run airline when you see the logo for Southwest Airlines. The Dell logo means direct mail computers to most people. The BMW logo on the back of a car instantly conveys a particular meaning to car aficionados. This brand equity is often the result of a company possessing a distinctive competency that it has been able to exploit over time.

Relating Distinctive Competencies to Business Opportunities

As we noted at the beginning of this chapter, not all apparent opportunities are real business opportunities and not all business opportunities should be exploited. Which ones should you pursue and which ones should you abandon? In general, you should select business opportunities in those areas where you possess some unique or special advantage over competitors. In other words, you should focus on opportunities for which your company has distinctive competencies.

The significance of this point is often overlooked or misunderstood. Managers frequently believe that if a relevant business opportunity is present, they should try to capitalize on it even though it may be a poor use of the firm's resources. However, a number of competitors may be about to respond to the same opportunity and some of them may be better able to do so. To commit to an area in which a firm is at a definite competitive disadvantage from the outset is poor business sense. Areas in which a business possesses a meaningful competitive edge over its competitors are the areas that it should emphasize.

Opportunity Cost

The "opportunity cost" of an investment in a new venture idea is the best alternative use of the capital. If a company invests a million dollars in one project, it must consider where else it could invest that million dollars and what return it would bring.

In addition, leaders of growing businesses must be sure that pursuing new opportunities will not threaten the main mission and focus of their businesses. In other words, an opportunity may exist and your business may have the capacity to act on it, but you may decide that doing so threatens your business in some important way.

Sustainable Competencies

Anything you can do to sustain a competence and prevent competitors from encroaching on your territory will go far in ensuring success for your business.

It is one thing to have or develop a distinctive competence. It is quite another to maintain it. The more successful your company is because of a competence, the more competitors will attempt to imitate or improve on it. Anything you can do to sustain a competence and prevent competitors from encroaching on your territory will go far in ensuring success for your business. Actions that can sustain a competence include patenting a product or process, keeping formulas for products secret, advertising the product heavily to develop brand loyalty, and developing unique containers and catchy slogans or product names that encourage customers to identify with the particular product or company.

122

Some companies go to great lengths to protect distinctive competencies. This is especially true when considering either retail or apparel brands. For example, Columbia Sportswear has a well-earned reputation for prosecuting or threatening to prosecute violators of its clothing designs that are protected by patents.

Few competencies are sustainable forever. Even Southwest Airlines, still the country's only consistently profitable airline, has faced growing competition from other low-frills airlines. In fact, JetBlue Airways was started in 2000 by a former executive of Southwest Airlines. It is also a no-frills airline, but it features newer planes and leather seats. Thus, in the markets where the two airlines overlap, Southwest's characteristics of no-frills, quick turnaround, and fun-loving employees is no longer a distinctive competence when considering JetBlue and a few others.

Sometimes normal evolutionary changes take away a company's distinctive competencies. Perhaps a company outperforms competitors because of a unique strength. Over time, competitors develop similar or even better competitive weapons. Those changes often occur slowly over time, so that no one really notices the changes. For example, changes in relative competitive strengths occur repeatedly among real estate companies in medium-sized cities. For a few years, one company dominates sales of real estate in a community; a few years later, another firm leads the pack; still later, another will take over as number one. A real estate firm is able to ward off competitors for a few years because of its size or because its key executives are well known in the city. The success of that firm, however, eventually fades when a competitor tries some other approach that customers find appealing. The tenuous nature of distinctive competencies should prompt you to search for ways to sustain your competencies.

Distinctive Competencies and Planning for Growth

The determination or recognition of your company's distinctive competencies is one of the critical, culminating events of the analysis phase of strategic planning.

The determination or recognition of your company's distinctive competencies is one of the critical, culminating events of the analysis phase of strategic planning. The distinctive competencies of the business become the focus or driving force behind selecting relevant business opportunities, preparing mission and goal statements, and planning strategic actions.

As we have said throughout this chapter, distinctive competencies can take the form of either resources (something the company has) or capabilities (something the firm does). You must develop not only distinctive competencies but also complementary sources of distinctive competencies. If you can develop a resource as a distinctive competence, let's say a superior product, then you must develop capabilities (e.g., processes) that support the product. If you can't develop both types of distinctive competencies—resources and capabilities—not only will this limit your company's ability to exploit opportunities, but it may also make it easy for competitors to imitate the competencies.

Consider EMI, Ltd., the company that introduced the CAT scanner, a machine used by the medical profession to detect cancer, among other things. (In fact, the EMI research engineer who invented the machine won a Nobel Prize in 1979 for doing so.) Initially, EMI was the only company that knew how to make CAT scanners and thus it clearly possessed a tangible resource (technology) as a source of distinctive competence. Unfortunately, however, it did not have the capabilities (service and support staff) to exploit its resource. General Electric, with its sophisticated manufacturing processes and a sizable sales force, saw the opportunity for CAT scanner sales. GE manufactured a modified version of EMI's invention (to work around the patent) and eventually benefited most from the machine.[2]

Competitive Weaknesses

Growth-oriented companies must focus on the future and the opportunities to be captured, but must not lose sight of signs of weakness.

As suggested by the EMI story above, it is important to keep an eye open for problems as you look for strengths and opportunities. Growth-oriented companies must, of course, focus on the future and the opportunities to be captured, but must not lose sight of signs of weakness.

Although careful analysis both of possible opportunities and your own strengths allows you to identify areas of distinctive competence, it may also suggest areas of competitive weakness—that is, areas of vulnerability in which competitors have a meaningful edge. In a highly competitive situation, one firm's distinctive competency is often another firm's competitive weakness. Just as distinctive competencies are developed over time, competitive weaknesses evolve over time.

Actions a company has taken or failed to take throughout its life can accrue into competitive weaknesses. Once recognized, however, competitive weaknesses can motivate the strategy process. You should respond in order to minimize, mitigate, or overcome areas of distinctive weakness.

Here is another caveat: you have to be just as objective about analyzing weaknesses as you are about analyzing strengths. Managers of emerging companies are often enamored with their products and businesses but may have great difficulty in recognizing competitive weaknesses. This difficulty generally stems both from an unrealistic analysis of the competitive environment and from an inadequate internal analysis. Remember how we called Chapter 8 "Taking a Hard Look at Yourself." It sometimes is indeed hard to take this hard look, especially when weaknesses may exist. This is why it is so important that you be open and ready to accept and respond to the outcomes of the analysis. It is often easier to see opportunities outside and strengths inside than to see competitive weaknesses. You must be as objective as possible, citing factual information rather than relying on opinions or conjecture. Indeed, one or two key areas of competitive weaknesses can, if unrealized and unattended, destroy the base of strength derived from a series of distinctive competencies.

Putting It All Together

It may be useful now to repeat the steps or processes that make up the analysis phase of the strategic planning model. First, you determine your vision for the company. Opportunity analysis then yields a series of possible opportunities, which you compare with an analysis of your strengths and weaknesses to determine if they are in fact relevant business opportunities worth studying further. Additional analysis focusing on competitors and key internal strengths permits you to clearly recognize your distinctive competencies or pinpoint those most fruitful for development. Then, you evaluate relevant business opportunities in terms of recognized distinctive competencies. Those opportunities most consistent with your company's competencies are the ones that you actively pursue and become the focus for subsequent planning efforts.

Your business may succeed—at least for a while—without a specific distinctive competence. In particular, this may be true if consumer demand is strong in relation to industry supply. Simply presenting the product or service to a ready market ensures at least short-term success. However, if business returns are attractive and no barriers impede new entrants into the industry, there will undoubtedly be an eventual competitive shakeout. It is then that those businesses with firmly established competencies have the greatest likelihood of survival.

It is time now for you to move from the analysis phase of growth planning to the action phase. You have looked outside for opportunities and you have taken that hard look inside and concluded that there were some real opportunities that could be captured. You may have even found some distinctive competencies that will allow you to get a leg up on the competition. It is now time to move from thinking to doing. It is time now to consider what types of strategies can get you the growth you want.

Notes

1. "SS&C Technologies, Inc.," *The Wall Street Transcript*, August 2004; and www.ssctech.com.

2. As noted in Laurence G. Weinzimmer, *Fast Growth* (Chicago: Dearborn Trade, 2001).

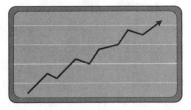

Chapter 12

Growth Strategies That Work

ZIPPO—NEARLY EVERYONE KNOWS THE ZIPPO BRAND NAME. YOU may have a Zippo lighter somewhere in your house. But after more than 70 years of producing lighters, Zippo Manufacturing Company is facing some tough challenges. Although the company still dominates the market for refillable lighters, that market is shrinking. Zippo, feeling the pinch of a general decline in smoking, realizes sales that are, at best, stagnant.

As we've seen in earlier chapters, this scenario can present some wonderful opportunities for creativity and progress. There is room for optimism and there can be growth. Of course, new strategies—growth strategies—are needed. And that seems to be the thinking of Zippo's chairman George Duke. Banking on its most dominant strength—a highly recognizable brand name—Duke decided to branch out. Moving carefully, the company's initial move was not a far stretch from its traditional lighters. Enter the Zippo Multi-Purpose Lighter. Producing a longer lighter made for fireplaces, lanterns, and grills, the company has been able to provide new uses for its traditional lighter and reach a whole different set of customers. It has, in essence, extended its brand.

What's next? Recognizing a new arena for growth, Zippo is now moving into grills and outdoor accessories. They even have plans to extend their

127

product line further to include camping equipment and outdoor gear.[1] They have carefully pieced together some fundamental and effective growth strategies that really do work.

Let's be clear. This chapter offers you no magic formula. But we do present some solid strategies that can help you realize the growth you are looking to gain. The particular growth strategy or set of strategies you choose will depend largely on the strengths and weaknesses of your business and the nature of your business environment. The growth strategy becomes your way of positioning your business to build on your competencies, exploit strengths and opportunities, and mitigate weaknesses and competitive threats.

Often, businesses fail to develop an overall growth strategy. There are a lot of reasons why that may happen. Some leaders lack a view of the opportunities that lie "just around the next corner." Others see potential, but don't have a plan for getting there. They emphasize short-term goals and operational decisions. And here is the unfortunate outcome: their future evolves as a reflection of past actions. Translation: they keep repackaging the past and they fail to shape a new and profitable future for their business. We want you to move beyond this ever-so-present danger.

Before You Set a Strategy ...

Establishing a growth strategy can be pretty heady stuff for most of us. It's even tougher to bring a leadership team together and get the members to agree on an appropriate strategy to pursue. So, before we even begin to look at some of growth options, let's begin with some basic assumptions that everyone needs to consider and understand.

First assumption—you are building for the future. Growth strategies are future strategies. They are decidedly proactive, not reactive. They are approaches to help you move from where you are today to some desired future. You'll have some people in the business who will pull you back to the past by their heavy reliance on historical data—the "here's what's worked and why" approach. As we have already discussed, historical data are important. It would be foolish and negligent to ignore such data. So use historical data as a tool, but keep your focus on the future.

Second assumption—focus on customers. Most businesses focus more on their competitors than on the customers. Growth strategies begin with the customer in mind. Growth strategies begin with knowing what's important to customers. How can we better meet customer needs? How can we reach untapped potential customers? How can we provide products or services that will encourage customers to choose us?

Third assumption—focus on opportunities. Many businesses construct strategies to stave off threats posed by either the competition or shifts in the environment. Such defensive moves may be necessary at times. But you are much better off at this juncture to look for opportunities. Be innovative here. Failures can be opportunities. Customer complaints can be opportunities. Look for problems that need solving. They are always the foundations of new growth.

Fourth assumption—you can grow. You're going to get broadsided by a lot of naysayers, so it's best to be ready. Some will argue that the market is saturated and growth potential is nil. If that's the case, you need to think about those markets and customers and what can be done differently to affect the landscape. Some will argue that your markets are mature and simply can't support growth of any magnitude. Don't fall prey to that line of thinking. You can grow, even in mature markets. Just ask Zippo Manufacturing Company.

Fifth assumption—don't take yourself too seriously. This may hit a little close to home, but we've seen it over and over again. You've invested a lot of time, energy, and (most likely) money in the business. You've played a major role in whatever success the business has experienced. Moving ahead or moving in new directions can be a real stab at your ego. Inevitably, any discussion of growth may feel like a collective admission that what you've done is not good enough. You may feel defensive as growth discussions begin to take shape. The funny thing here is that you will know, at least at an intellectual level, that the discussions and arguments being tossed around are healthy. But, at a personal level, you can still feel like all your hard work is unappreciated.

Your people may be nervous and tentative about suggesting new ideas precisely because they are uncertain of how you will react. If you seem defensive, they will pick up those cues clearly and immediately. You can then expect productive, growth-oriented discussions to take a rapid and silent detour. So, check that ego. Encourage criticism coupled with a "better way." And don't take yourself too seriously.

Ted Hoff was one the inventors of the microprocessor when he was at Intel. He praises Intel's management for its approach to customers. "We didn't do what the customer wanted. We did something better."[2]

Going for Growth: The Big Picture

Growth strategies can focus markets, products, or a combination of the two. Figure 12-1 shows how going after markets and products yields different growth strategies. Your business can realize growth by using a focus strategy, a market development strategy, a product development strategy, or a diversification strategy. Let's look at each of these options in more detail.

Market

	Existing	New
Existing	**Focus Strategies** • Product niche • Market niche	**Market Development Strategies** • Internal development • Franchising • Strategic alliance
New	**Product Development Strategies** • Incremental • Radical	**Diversification Strategies** • Related • Unrelated

Product

Figure 12-1. Topology of growth strategies

Doing What We Do Best: Focus Strategies

The most common growth strategy is the focus strategy. With this strategy, you emphasize existing products or services in your existing markets. You pursue growth by sticking to what you know and do the best. There is solid logic to this approach to growth. You will be working in areas where you already have experience. Therefore, you probably have a good understanding of the overall market situation.

When using a focus strategy, you will emphasize a single product and market niche. As a result, you and your managers can be geared toward a very central and streamlined set of issues. In short, you are more likely to stay on top of important market changes.

An example of a focus strategy is seen in Kurzweil Educational Systems, a company started by Ray Kurzweil in 1996. The company sells educational software—what is known as assistive technology—for visually impaired students and students with learning disabilities. Their products work by scanning virtually any printed document into a PC and converting the text into speech. For example, the Kurzweil 3000 is designed for people with learning disabilities and reading disabilities. The software presents readers with an image of an entire page and then reads each word aloud in a realistic-sounding synthesized voice.

The company focuses on a single market—people with disabilities. And it focuses on a single product line—educational software that converts text to speech. Today, the company is thriving and Kurzweil is recognized as a leader in the assistive technology industry.[3]

The focus strategy is often popular with smaller businesses. Smaller businesses that remain flexible and adaptable can zero in on the special needs of their target market. And they can address those needs more quickly than can their larger counterparts.

Further, smaller businesses can experience growth by exploiting opportunities that are normally overlooked or bypassed by larger firms. Those pockets of opportunity can generate amazing growth.

Jim Murdock saw the opportunity when he founded Endless Pools. His concept was simple, but what he developed may be the ultimate in exercise equipment. The pool is relatively small, needing only an 8-by-15-foot space. The pool provides a smooth and adjustable current for swimming or other aquatic exercise. Murdock emphasizes the quality of his product, especially the design and manufacturing. To help ensure consistent quality, he uses no local distributors. Each pool is sold factory-direct. To help acquaint potential customers with the product, the company maintains a list of owners in various locations who are willing to let serious potential customers try out the pool. Think about the market—exercise-conscious folks. Think about the potential—baby boomers whose aging bodies demand they step away from weight-bearing forms of exercise. Think of the product that is continually being fine-tuned and improved. In a few short years, Endless Pools has seen revenues top $25 million and it has sold to customers in every state, as well as in 25 countries throughout the world.[4]

Of course, relying solely on a focus strategy can be risky. If the present product or market remains strong, the strategy can lead to substantial growth. But if either the product or the market loses its vitality, the business is on tenuous ground and may need some repositioning. We think back to Mark Twain's caveat: "Put all your eggs in one basket and guard the basket."

"Now more than ever, consumers want to support companies they trust and that are honest with them. I think the past year has shown us that the size of the company and its quarterly earnings don't necessarily guarantee winning in the end."

—Gary Erickson, Owner and CEO, Clif Bar Inc.[5]

Let's Stretch a Bit: Market Development Strategies

Seventeen Studio Spa Salon, in Plano, Texas, caters to a young crowd. Their original target market was 12- to 34-year-old girls and young women who wanted everything from traditional hair styling to acne facials. But the business recognized an untapped and potentially lucrative market—teenage boys. According to co-owner Susan Tierney, the boys enjoy the "cool" atmosphere of the studio and "they get to see the girls." Today, teenage boys are 20 percent of their customers. Experiencing healthy sales, the business hopes to continue its growth by expanding to as many as 150 new locations by 2010.[6]

Market development strategies achieve growth by extending existing products and services into new markets.

Seventeen Studio Spa Salon is using the time-honored growth strategy of market development. Market development strategies achieve growth by extending existing products and services into new markets. These strategies can be of two types—*geographic expansion* and *new target markets*. Actually, both types were used at Seventeen. Let's look a bit more closely at each type.

In geographic expansion, the product or service remains unchanged. In a similar vein, the business continues to emphasize the same customer and product characteristics that have brought past success. However, new geographic markets for existing lines are identified and tapped. As we saw with Seventeen, their concept proved to be successful, so they plan to open additional facilities in other locations.

The second method of market development is selling the same or similar products to new target markets. Seventeen did this when they recognized and appealed to the market for teenage boys.

Examples abound. Consider the financial services industry. Many companies have gained growth by zeroing in on large, lucrative, but underserved markets. So, today we see companies that offer a full range of services but focus on specific markets. One business may target investments for professional women, while another emphasizes financial planning for baby boomers who are approaching retirement.

One of the key advantages of a market development strategy is that you can maintain a high degree of consistency and stability. For example, if your business has used a focus strategy successfully, you might be able to capture new markets using the same products or services.

Taking a solid or winning product or service into new markets makes a lot of sense. Although the idea seems basic, the execution can be tricky. As the old saying goes, "The devil's in the details." As a business expands geographically, it has to have a plan for ensuring the talent needed to support the growth. There must also be careful checks that quality and service do not slide from one location to another. In short, your management task becomes more complicated.

Therefore, we need to look at some options to market development. In most cases, your market development growth will follow one of three paths—internal development, franchising, or strategic alliance. A closer look at each is warranted.

All on Your Own: Internal Development

Internal development is an approach to implementing a market development strategy where you enter new markets all on your own. You will identify new locations; provide the necessary capital, equipment, and people; and oversee the management of the new facilities.

There are three major advantages. First, you have control: you say how the new location will operate. Second, all profits are kept by the business: you don't have to share them with partners. Third, you may be able to realize economies of scale as you lower your average cost of operations by increasing the size of your production or service facilities and your production volume.

There are two major disadvantages to expanding markets through internal development. First, it can be very expensive: you may not have the money to finance this approach. Second, you have to be sure you understand the unique features of the new markets where you want to locate. We have seen situations where a great concept did not play well in a new market because of unexpectedly strong customer loyalty to a locally owned competitor.

When thought through and done carefully, market development through internal growth can be a very successful. Often, it is a logical next move if your focus strategy has worked well. Consider the example of D.G. Yuengling & Sons.

Founded in 1829, this six-generation family business is America's oldest brewery. For most of its 175-year history, Yuengling refused to pursue a strategy of growth, preferring to focus on its small but solid Pennsylvania-based markets. By building strong and loyal local markets, the company survived while many similar breweries failed. In part, it thrived because of its exclusive, somewhat cult-like status.

Internal development is an approach to implementing a market development strategy where you enter new markets all on your own.

133

All this changed when Dick Yuengling took over the business in 1985. He decided to grow and expand, but his approach was careful and strategic. He moved slowly into one new market at a time and built a following. This strategy allowed the company to expand from its Pennsylvania base to nine other states along the Atlantic and the Gulf and the District of Columbia. Sales have rocketed and the company has experienced double-digit growth in an industry that generally has been stable and non-expansive. Has this worked? Even though its beer is sold in only 11 states, Yuengling is the country's fifth-largest brewery, shipping over a million barrels (over 400 million bottles) annually.[7]

Crystal Rug Cleaners was started in an exclusive section of Florida's Gulf Coast in the early 1990s by Michael Richards. Richards began with a careful assessment of the market and the opportunities it posed. First, income levels were extremely high and homes were large and expensive. The carpeting was high quality, often including expensive Oriental carpets. Although there were a number of cleaning firms in the area, none had established itself as emphasizing care and quality and none focused exclusively on carpets. Richards reasoned that the upper-income market was reluctant to entrust its cleaning needs to most of the cleaning firms, particularly since incorrect cleaning methods could damage or ruin expensive carpets. Richards trained extensively in cleaning methods and techniques, emphasizing those unique to high-grade and Oriental carpets. To highlight his competence and expertise, Richards confined the company's activities solely to carpet and rug cleaning. By distinguishing himself from his competitors and focusing on a single product/market orientation, Richards saw his business grow and prosper.

Within three years, Richards had saturated his current market, thus diminishing the opportunity for additional growth. Using excess profits, he decided to establish satellite operations in nearby communities, offering the same services that had already proven to be successful. The expansion did not occur piecemeal. It was carefully planned. Richards projected demand for each new market and budgeted his costs and returns accordingly. The business continued to grow and the company's foundations of service, professionalism, and expertise were maintained.

Be sure that when you address new markets you do not forget or confuse the needs of established markets.

There is a final caveat to offer here. Be sure that when you address new markets you do not forget or confuse the needs of established markets. Many leaders make the mistake of becoming so enamored with the excitement of new markets that they ignore their traditional base of strength. Be aware of this danger and guard against it.

Growth by Association: Franchising

If you don't have the resources to pursue market development on your own or if you are looking for rapid expansion, franchising may be considered. Perhaps you've never thought about franchising your business. It's not for everyone and certainly not for every situation. But it can be a great avenue for growth.

Consider just a few examples. Precision Door Services, Inc. had a great concept and was convinced it could be "the best garage door company in America." It used franchising to expand to 50 locations across the U.S. in less than three years.[8] Or what about Jet-Black®? Jet-Black is exclusively a seal-coating service business that provides customers "the world's most beautiful driveways." After five years in business, the company's methods were refined and customer demand was overwhelming. Founders Doug and Andy Hoiland knew they had to expand; franchising was the approach they chose. They awarded their first franchise in 1993. Today, there are 85 franchise owners in over 135 territories in the U.S. and Canada and Jet-Black is rated as the top asphalt maintenance franchise by *Entrepreneur* Magazine.[9] The story is similar for Two Men and a Truck®. The company started when brothers Brig and Jon Sorber began moving people with an old pickup truck while in high school in the early 1980s. When the boys left for college, demand for their services continued and their mother, Mary Ellen Sheets, decided to step up the business in 1985. Today, with over 140 franchise locations in 26 states, Two Men and a Truck is the first and largest franchised local moving company.[10]

In all these cases, the formula is similar. First, there is a proven and successful business concept. Don't lose sight of this point. Franchising is a way to grow a business that is already a winner. Your capacity to attract franchisees depends both on the record of success you have already attained and the likelihood of replicating the success in new locations. Second, the concept, approach, and methods must be packaged as a system that others can follow. In other words, franchisees are really paying for your business's name, but they also need the methods, training, and support that will ensure their success. Franchisors often provide extensive networks of support. Further, franchisors often provide special equipment; unique, company-specific products; advertising help; and extensive and regular training. This helps assure you that consistency and quality will be in place. And it helps assure you that franchise holders will succeed.

Becoming a franchisor has several advantages. Although the initial costs to set up a franchising system can be high, once the system is in place, fewer

Franchising is a way to grow a business that is already a winner.

135

resources are required to develop new markets. Second, because markets can be developed faster, economies of scale can be achieved in areas such as advertising, distribution, and product development. Third, selling franchises highly motivates owners of individual franchises, who generally invest considerable funds and time to make their franchise work. Further, as the number of units grows, the franchise system grows in both visibility and respectability as customers and potential customers are increasingly exposed to the business.

The major disadvantage is a loss of direct control. You do everything you can to ensure that franchise holders are competent and dedicated, but they exercise great independence over their operations. You may also consider it a disadvantage that, apart from the initial franchise fee and royalties you receive (this can vary a great deal), others are getting rich on your business. This is not the way to approach franchising. You choose the franchising option because growth potential is high, but you have neither the resources nor the desire to build the new markets on your own. Franchising should be a carefully selected arrangement that benefits all who are involved.

We Can Help Each Other: Strategic Alliances

In a strategic alliance, two or more businesses share resources or capabilities in areas where each is distinctly qualified.

Here is a common scenario. You want to aggressively pursue market development. But after assessing your firm's relative competitive strengths, you realize you don't have the all the resources or all the capabilities you need to make it work. In such an instance, you may be tempted to forgo pursuit of a potentially attractive market opportunity. There is another possibility. Consider forming a strategic alliance with one or more other firms.

In a strategic alliance, two or more businesses share resources or capabilities in areas where each is distinctly qualified. And that is the key. Businesses choose to work with each other when their strengths complement each other. The alliance allows partners to share costs and move forward in a highly efficient manner, but it works only when each partner brings valued strengths to the alliance and can trust other participants to do their part.

Some strategic alliances are well known. For example, the United Airlines alliance with Starbucks allows you to have gourmet coffee as you cruise the skies. Many businesses use the alliance as a matter of necessity when trying to move from current markets into new markets. For example, Copeland Corporation had a solid business that focused on air conditioning and commercial refrigeration products. However, its alliance with Kirloskar, India's largest compressor manufacturer, gave Copeland entry into a large and lucrative new market.[11]

Be careful when pursuing the strategic alliance option. Strategic alliances often seem attractive, but they are difficult to manage. In fact, recent studies indicate that most fail: "A majority of alliances, 55 percent, fall apart within three years after they are formed."[12] You have to be sure the businesses appreciate one another and can work together.

Make It Better: Product Development Strategies

In contrast to market development, product development strategies stress variations or improvements in your firm's products. These new products are then introduced to your existing markets, in the hope that the positive image customers have of current products will carry over to the new products. This growth strategy can be pursued through either *incremental* or *radical* product development.

With incremental product development, your business modifies its existing products and maintains and targets current markets and present customers (with assumed loyalty) as it introduces the product variations. Remember: incremental product development yields variations and improvements, but no overall change in the basic product.

Radical product development, on the other hand, seeks so novel an alteration of your existing product that a totally new or different product is created. The current products are not eliminated. Growth comes from sales of both the new product and the original. Consider cell phones as an example. Many people simply want a standard cell phone. But others long for the latest souped-up version. So now you can get a slick cell phone with e-mail capabilities, an organizer, a camera, and just about any business application you want.

In some cases, new products dwarf the success of original products. Steve Demos is founder and president of White Wave. After dabbling with success with a number of soy-based products, Demos made a radical product move. He introduced a soymilk product called Silk. Tapping a growing market, Silk has experienced amazing growth. Today, over eight million households purchase the product annually and nearly every supermarket carries it.[13]

A product development strategy may be adopted by service companies as well as by manufacturers. One reason product development is so attractive is the possibility it offers for high returns. Introducing new services or products can bring big profits—at least until competitors recognize and

Incremental product development yields variations and improvements, but no overall change in the basic product.

137

respond to the changes. But there are also significant risks. Being on the cutting edge demands a careful and accurate reading of environmental trends, as well as a timely and cost-effective response.

Busting Out: Diversification Strategies

When you decide to pursue a diversification strategy, you are stretching into new areas of business.

When you decide to pursue a diversification strategy, you are stretching into new areas of business. In terms of our previous discussion, you are entering new markets with new products. You are not ignoring your original or core business activities. In fact, those activities may still command the bulk of your resources and energy. But you are extending into other products or services and markets.

The logic behind this strategic move usually has one of two bases. First, you may decide that there are excellent opportunities for continued and expanded growth by moving into additional areas of business. Or second, you may be concerned about the growth potential of your primary business. In particular, if dark clouds are gathering over your business, diversification may be a way to offset a downturn or stagnation and allow you to continue growing.

Let's begin with an important distinction. Diversification can be of two types—*related* or *unrelated*.

In related diversification, the new business has some common link or tie to the existing business. We refer to this tie as *strategic fit*. Strategic fit is a key to related diversification because it allows you capitalize on strengths you already have established.

Consider a software development company that concentrates exclusively on educational software. Given that the business has mastered the software development process, it seems logical to look for ways to expand this expertise into new products and markets. So the company decides to create a line of financial software. Even though the specific market and the nature of the products are quite different, there is strategic fit since the basic product—software development—is being transferred from one business to another.

Let's look at another example. As the name suggests, Closets By Design® started in 1982 with a single focus—providing busy families the answer to closet clutter. The business had a unique approach. It offered in-home consultation, custom closet designs, top-quality products and workmanship, and a lifetime warranty. Not surprisingly, as the number of time- conscious, dual-career families grew, so did the business success of Closets By Design.

138

Building from its core base of expertise, the company decided to grow through careful, related diversification. You can probably think of some logical areas for expansion. So could the owners. They have extended their business into organizing garages, home offices, entertainment centers, and home executive offices. Now they have even branched out into doing commercial offices. As you can see, they have tapped new markets and added new products. But the same original concept that brought success is still being applied.[14]

Let's contrast our discussion of related diversification with the second type of diversification—unrelated. As the name suggests, here you decide to pursue an appealing growth opportunity even though the new business is unrelated to your existing business. This strategy has a major business advantage. You avoid putting all your eggs in one basket.

We see this often. Consider the owner of a successful insurance business who realizes that his cash flow could underwrite additional business ventures. As a hedge against the volatility and increased regulation of the insurance industry, he decides to spread his risks by investing in a restaurant franchise. Totally unrelated businesses, no real strategic fit, but it's conceivably a wise growth move.

It's probably not hard to see that related diversification is generally a safer strategy than unrelated diversification. It is less risky to stretch into a new business opportunity where strategic fit allows you to build on your experience and established competence. We have seen a number of businesses stray into totally new territory and commit considerable time, energy, and resources to their new ventures. Often, their established, core business suffered. Consequently, we encourage you to look, at least initially, for related options. We are not minimizing the value of unrelated diversification or the growth it may offer. We are being realistic and recognizing the higher level of risk that is involved.

Michael Holigan is president of Holigan Family Holdings Ltd. and host of the syndicated television show, *Michael Holigan's Your New House*. His diversification plan is straightforward. He wants "to expand into any and every product and service a person might need" when remodeling or even building a home. He wants the typical home remodeler to think of him and he wants to have the answers they need.[15]

Which Way Do You Go to Grow? Selecting the Right Growth Strategy

Given the four general growth strategies we've just discussed, which option do you select? Which is the right growth strategy for you? As you might expect, clear, easy answers are rare and exceptions are common. However, two factors will help you determine which strategy is most appropriate—the growth potential of your company's industry and your business's relative competitive strength. Industry growth potential should be not only assessed in the present, but projected over your firm's planning horizon. A careful and thorough environmental analysis should provide enough information to decide if industry growth potential is relatively strong or relatively weak. It is the interplay of industry growth and competitive strengths that determines your selection of strategy.

High-Growth Industries

The most appropriate strategy for a business in an industry with high growth potential is generally to continue with a focus strategy.

The most appropriate strategy for a business in an industry with high growth potential is generally to continue with a focus strategy. In this case, rather than expanding into new areas, you should invest resources into your current industry to achieve future growth. The logic is straightforward. There is ample opportunity for growth and you can play on your proven strength and expertise.

A market development or product development strategy may be effective under high-growth conditions, but be careful before using either of these strategies. You should consider product or market development only if you have distinctive competencies that can be applied to the new products or markets.

If you find yourself in a high-growth market but you don't have sufficient resources to capture that market alone, franchising or strategic alliances can be helpful strategies. In short, you can continue to grow by partnering with others. Partnering through franchising allows your business to be replicated over and over with franchisees. And a strategic alliance with another business can provide assistance in the manufacture and/or distribution of your products.

Businesses following a focus or strategic alliance strategy typically have competitive strengths or distinctive competencies. However, if your industry is growing, you may be able to achieve significant growth without any dominant competitive strengths. Demand may simply be so strong that any firm able to deliver the desired product to customers will succeed and grow. Because such a rosy condition is always temporary, be careful here. Eventually, industry growth will begin to stabilize and subside. Those businesses without competitive strengths and distinctive competencies will be most vulnerable. So, emphasizing company strengths during times of growth is a wise and prudent thing to do.

Low-Growth Industries

Market development and product development strategies are appropriate when your analysis of the industry indicates that growth is tapering off or will be soon. Here you should capitalize on one or more of your business's competitive strengths to expand and grow. This expansion may be through developing new products to sell to existing markets—product development. Or you may find ways to sell your current products to new markets—market development. In either case, these moves should allow your sales to increase in spite of slowing industry growth.

If industry growth is clearly on the wane, you should consider diversification. Take another look at your environment and determine whether your business has competitive strengths that can be applied in new areas. As we have already discussed, diversification holds considerable risks. Look for areas of related diversification. Assess whether you can build upon and transfer your company's strengths, in terms of concept, processes, or products. Then carefully redirect your firm's efforts to new products and target markets while keeping ties to your current business. This formula has been a winner for Zippo, Closets By Design, and scores of other progressive operations.

If industry growth is clearly on the wane, you should consider diversification.

For most smaller and midsized businesses, unrelated diversification is the right move in only a few rare circumstances. Unrelated diversification may be a necessary defensive move if you feel your current industry is threatened. This strategy can be an appropriate offensive move if you feel that you need to invest excess funds outside the current industry. This form of diversification makes sense when government regulation threatens an industry or when demographics or other social changes signal severe problems or concerns about the prospect of future growth.

An example of this occurred regarding a small local bakery/restaurant business. The low-carb craze and new competition from a chain restaurant forced the business to diversify into a strategic alliance with another company that sold meats via catalog and the Internet. The bakery owner benefited from having her products available to a new market and from having access to the meat business for her restaurant business.

Putting It into Practice

When deciding on the right growth strategy, you must assess both your growth potential and your growth-related opportunities. Remember that growth potential is a function of environmental factors, internal strengths and weaknesses, and your own views of what you want and how fast you wish to move.

Above all, keep in mind the importance of controlled growth. Most businesses want to grow. Growth is exciting and challenging and provides you a sense of prestige. These are the wrong reasons for pursuing growth.

Be sure you have a rational, bottom-line business case for pursuing growth. Strip away the emotion as much as you can and take a hard, honest look at that business case. Remember that the underlying logic for pursuing growth is to improve your company's long-term competitive position and long-term profitability.

When you decide to grow, you have to commit resources to make that growth possible. In the short run, growth may not lead to higher profits.

Keep in mind that growth usually brings some sacrifices. One short-term sacrifice may be profit. Growing businesses may have impressive revenue growth. Profitability, however, may be at the same level or even lower than it was before growth began. When you decide to grow, you have to commit resources to make that growth possible. In the short run, growth may not lead to higher profits.

There are other risks to growth. For example, be careful that as you grow you do not ignore the business practices that made you successful. We have seen companies that established strong and loyal customer bases because of their excellent service. However as they grew and employees became focused on keeping up with demand, service eroded and so did their reputation for service excellence.

Again, the key is controlled growth. Rather than looking at "growing fast," consider emphasizing "growing as fast as you can." The difference requires perspective and balance. You are balancing resources allocated for growth and resources allocated for effectively "managing growth."

Notes

1. Ellen Neuborne, "Case Study," *Inc.,* September 2004, pp. 42-44.
2. "Inspiring Innovation," *Harvard Business Review*, August 2002.

3. www.kurzweiledu.com (accessed August 28, 2004).

4. www.endlesspools.com (accessed June 23, 2004).

5. "The Experts Weigh In," (reactions to Nicole Gull, "Just Say Om" [case study]) *Inc.*, July 2003, p. 44.

6. Chris Pentilla, "Hot Biz: Spas," *Entrepreneur* Magazine, December 2003, p. 85.

7. Rod Kurtz, "America's Oldest Brewery," *Inc.*, July 2004, p. 64.

8. www.precisiondoor.net (accessed September 3, 2004).

9. www.jet-black.com (accessed September 4, 2004).

10. www.twomenandatruck.com (accessed September 4, 2004).

11. Ed Rigsbee, *Developing Strategic Alliances*, Chapter 1: "What's in It for Me?" www.rigsbee.com (accessed September 5, 2004).

12. Karen E. Klein, "Urge to Merge? Take Care to Beware," *Business Week Online*, June 28, 2004, accessed October 29, 2004.

13. Susan Greco, "1+1+1= The New Mass Market," *Inc.*, January 2003, p. 32.

14. www.closetsbydesign.com (accessed September 14, 2004).

15. Geoff Williams, "It's Really Something Else," *Entrepreneur* Magazine, February 2003, pp. 60-63.

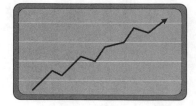

Chapter 13

Setting the "Right" Goals to Make Things Happen

I
N OPERATION FOR LESS THAN TEN YEARS, eBAY HAS TRULY BECOME THE "world's online marketplace." The company has helped define the way technology can revolutionize the marketplace. The challenges it has faced have been daunting, but its impact has been nothing short of dramatic. And, believe it or not, eBay has earned another impressive distinction: it is the fastest-growing company in history. Much of the credit goes to Meg Whitman, eBay's president and CEO. In fact, Whitman was recently named by *Fortune* magazine as the most powerful woman in business today!

Under Whitman's watch, active users of the company's services have rocketed to 48 million. Revenues have jumped to over $3 billion. And with its lean, Internet-based infrastructure, operating income now exceeds $1 billion. The company has clear strategies for continued growth. These include expanding into new international markets, making key investments in technology, and offering more online tools.[1]

But these strategies come alive with the business's goals. While flexible and innovative, eBay recognizes the need for strong financial discipline. You can expect clear expectations for increases in the number of active users, the number of listings, sales growth, and profit margins, to name only a few areas. These markers provide focus and help the company evaluate its progress and make corrective moves. In short, clear, specific, and challenging goals help make things happen.

You have defined your strategies for growth. Those strategies have been the product of a careful analysis of your firm's capabilities and its environment. Building these strategies has been your first action step. But simply determining broad strategies is not enough. These strategies must be converted into goals for the business as a whole and for the units within the business. Setting specific goals—the right goals—for your business is the focus of this chapter. As you and your people accept and work toward these goals, you'll begin to see results. Hopefully, those results will be impressive, like the results experienced by eBay.

Why You Need the Right Goals

Suppose you and a friend are leisurely driving around the city some Sunday afternoon and you recognize that you have no idea where you are. Are you lost? The answer is no. But suppose one of you realizes, "It's four o'clock! We were supposed to be at a meeting 15 minutes ago!" Now you are lost.

The leisurely drive was fine as long as the only goal was to have a good time. However, once you realized you had to be somewhere at a certain time and you were late, you looked around for landmarks or asked directions. The point is that only if you have a specific goal to strive for do you take the actions necessary to achieve it.

This analogy speaks clearly to businesses. One of the fundamental dangers for growing businesses is that they simply "drive around," serving customers and working at a frenetic pace but lacking clarity of direction. Business goals provide the needed clarity and direction. Once a goal is set, performance can be measured in terms of that goal. Thus, a goal is simultaneously a planning tool and a control tool—a planning tool because it must precede the development of a plan and a control tool because it is a preset standard against which performance can be measured. If goals are not being achieved, corrective steps may be taken to improve performance.

Goals also motivate employees. Achievable goals, in fact, can become a rallying point for the entire company. Recently, the owner of a small manufacturing firm attributed her firm's ability to weather some tough economic and competitive times to the fact that the employees knew where the company was headed. They knew what the owners expected and had a good

One of the fundamental dangers for growing businesses is that they simply "drive around," serving customers and working at a frenetic pace but lacking clarity of direction.

sense of what was likely to happen. She noted that sharing goals built a sense of identity and was convinced that the open sharing of goals fostered a "we are in this together" spirit that helped the firm rebound from some bleak days.

SMART Goals

If goals are to have meaning and the process of goal setting is to work, certain basic rules, guidelines, or considerations must be noted. As you develop goals, be sure they are SMART goals. SMART is an acronym for the characteristics that goals should possess—*S*pecific, *M*easurable, *A*ttainable, *R*ealistic, and *T*angible.

Goal statements should be specific and clear and, to the extent possible, quantifiable or measurable.

Goal statements should be specific and clear and, to the extent possible, quantifiable or measurable. The clearer and more precise the goal, the greater the likelihood that it will be pursued and attained. It is simplistic to say that you cannot control what you do not measure. Yet if you want high levels of performance from your people, they have to understand precisely what end result is expected. General platitudes are not acceptable. In fact, to be most useful, goals should be cast in terms of percentage increases from a baseline. Thus, a goal of a 5 percent increase in sales over last year is better than saying that we want to increase sales next month.

Effective goal statements should also be challenging yet attainable and realistic. Challenging goals are essential for growing businesses. Goals that are too simple or too easily reached cheat the business of its full potential. They can lead people to feel underutilized in their jobs and contribute to declines in morale and job satisfaction. On the other hand, goals that are too lofty may quickly be perceived as unreasonable or unrealistic and employees will not even try to achieve them.

Goal statements should be tangible and phrased in terms of outcomes or results rather than processes. Managers must focus on desired accomplishments, not activities to achieve these accomplishments. There is a world of difference between saying, "This week we will work on the budget," and "By the end of this week, the budget will be completed."

Finally, goals must be communicated throughout the organization. Regardless of how impressive a goal statement may be in meeting the foregoing criteria, its potential to influence behavior is lost if it is not communicated to employees. Many managers understand the value of open communication and include their employees in the goal-setting process, which not only improves the goals but also becomes a key to motivation.

Creating the "Right" Goals

Although setting solid goals is largely a judgmental process, it should not be done by the seat of your pants. In part, goal setting should be based on historical data, but to a greater extent it should be based on the analyses you've completed in your planning process.

The focus of goals may change from time to time. Suppose, for example, that sales have increased as planned over the past several years, but costs have risen dramatically. The goal for the next period may focus on cost containment. Sales increases may still be encouraged, but the primary emphasis will be on reducing expenses per sales dollar.

We recently worked with a business experiencing this scenario. The company's leaders were pleased that revenue goals were being achieved. However, concern was building that escalating costs associated with those revenues were clouding the profit picture. Therefore, the leaders set a series of goals to streamline expenses while maintaining revenues. Bottom line: the company identified the right goals at the right time.

Often, a specific numerical goal will be a compromise among your key people. The marketing manager may suggest a target increase in sales of, say, 10 percent. The controller may be more pessimistic and feel that 6 percent is the most that could be expected. The production manager may be pretty sure that 7 percent or 8 percent is the maximum increase obtainable without a substantial capital outlay. You work with the managers. You must help bring balance and realism into your goals. Encourage each person to offer a sales forecast for the coming year along with related information. Together, you can establish final goals that are meaningful and acceptable. Open communication becomes a key to such goal-setting compromises.

Goal setting is one of those "rubber meets the road" activities. It's not as exciting as the discoveries that come from analysis. It's not as dramatic as locking on a new strategic direction. But if goal setting is not well done, little action is likely. And needed corrective moves are shrouded in confusion.

A Balancing Act

No business will have a single overriding goal. All groups, all businesses, and all individuals have multiple goals. Many of the goals are congruous, but some will be in conflict. For example, a goal to be a successful business owner sometimes conflicts with a goal to be a successful parent.

Your business may even have mutually exclusive goals. One manager may have a goal in conflict with another manager, or a manager may have two goals that conflict with each other. In either case, the exclusivity means that one cannot be achieved without serious damage to efforts to achieve the other. For both new and emerging businesses, conflict among goals can affect the strategy of the firm. One group of managers, for example, may want to commit funds to introduce the firm's products into new markets. Another group may be convinced that funds need to be allocated to technological improvements and product modifications to keep up with changes in the industry. Both groups argue that their goal is the best way for the business to achieve growth. Because funds are limited, both sets of goals cannot be pursued, so the conflicts must be resolved or internal dissension and indecision can cripple the business.

Stacking the Deck

Everyone establishes priorities because we can never attain all that we want to attain or do all that we want to do. Thus, we learn to prioritize and determine which of life's objectives are most important. Businesses too have multiple opportunities and multiple goals, and it is difficult, if not impossible, to achieve all of them. This is particularly true when growth presents an array of opportunities, making it necessary to set priorities for goals. You may decide that the major emphasis this year will be on hiring new employees because the major emphasis last year was on expanding into a new area. Sales may have increased dramatically, but now personnel needs must be addressed. Although growth and expansion received top priority last year, they now must take second place to human resource considerations. Identifying the right goals can improve your odds of implementing your strategy effectively.

Setting priorities for goals is particularly important in product development. If a firm has a number of products that could be marketed, it may decide that products A and B will receive attention and funding next year and products C, D, and E the following year. Similarly, the firm may budget to replace some old equipment this year and schedule the remainder for replacement two years from now.

Levels and Time Frames

Goal setting is often seen as a complex process. You may cringe at the thought of wading through the necessary procedures. This is unfortunate because goal setting doesn't have to be overly cumbersome.

All goals are not the same; there are different levels and types. While such distinctions may appear to complicate the goal-setting process, they are

Goals are important planning tools. But they may be even more important as control tools. Remember Alice's exchange with the Cheshire Cat. "Would you tell me, please, which way I ought to walk from here?" "That depends a good deal on where you want to go," said the Cat.[2]

the basis for a logical system that allows the power of strategic goal setting to emerge.

Levels of Goals

As noted in Figure 13-1, two levels of goals—company and unit—are typical. Company goals relate to the performance or accomplishments of the overall business. Unit goals relate to the performance or accomplishments of one or more departments or units within the business. Figure 13-2 shows how company and unit goals differ yet relate to each other. Company goals establish certain demands and requirements that need to be reflected in the unit goals.

For example, let's consider a manufacturing business that wants to secure a 5 percent growth in revenues (company goal). In order to meet the company goal, marketing must develop a more effective advertising and promotion scheme, operations must increase its capacity, the sales force must secure new contracts, and human resources must hire and train new workers. All these activities take place at the unit level. Unit goals, then, help your people see how their specialties fit into the overall business plan.

Now here is the key. Unit goals must mesh with one another and with the overall business goals. Unfortunately, contemporary business is plagued by the lack of integration of unit goals. For example, the marketing department may develop new promotional programs without much regard for how they affect other functional areas or the overall efficiency of the business. The marketing department may do an excellent job of securing new contracts or additional orders but, in the process, outsell the company's capac-

Company Goals
(Relate to performance or accomplishments in the overall business)

Unit Goals
(Relate to performance or accomplishments of each
functional area within the business)

| Advertising | Operations | Sales | Human Resources |

Figure 13-1. Company and unit goals

149

Company Goals
5% growth in revenues in the next fiscal year

Unit Goals

Advertising
Develop a new advertising and promotional approach to reach 30% more potential customers by 7/31

Sales
Reach and finalize 10% increase in contract sales by 7/31

Human Resources
Hire and train 20 new workers by 4/30. Relocate and train internal employees to meet advertising, production, and sales goals by 4/30

Operations
Increase production capacity and production runs to produce 20% more finished product by 8/31

Figure 13-2. How company and unit goals differ yet relate

Conflicts among goals will surely arise. These conflicts can even provide needed checks and balances. Yet, you must set priorities and help your people align goals so the business wins.

ity to produce on time. This condition is known as *suboptimization*. It simply means that one unit is succeeding but to the detriment of other units as well as the overall business. You must prevent suboptimization. Therefore, each unit must see itself as a part of the whole business. All must recognize that each part complements the others.

Keep in mind that company goals must precede unit goals. Company goals are established and communicated to units. Unit managers then develop goals and review them with you to ensure that they fit properly with other unit goals and make an appropriate, balanced contribution to the business goals. Make sure all managers are involved. They all need to see the way unit goals fit together and build to promote company goals.

Goal Time Frames

We typically establish goals within three time frames, as shown in Figure 13-3. These three time frames—horizon goals, near-term goals, and target goals—are interrelated and interdependent.

Horizon goals focus on accomplishments expected over the course of your firm's overall planning horizon. The longer-time nature of these goals

Horizon Goals
(Cover the firm's planning horizon)

↓

Near-Term Goals
(Cover the firm's next operating cycle)

↓

Target Goals
(Cover the short run, i.e., weeks or days)

Figure 13-3. Time frames for goals

means they involve relatively high levels of uncertainty. Horizon goals therefore tend to be broader and less specific than other types of goals.

Near-term goals are established to set results or accomplishments expected within the firm's next operating cycle. Although that period varies among industries and companies, normally near-term goals deal with the next six months to a year. Many companies refer to these goals as *short-term* goals and assume that they are for one year.

From a planning perspective, horizon goals should be established before other goals. Often there is a strong temptation to think of the shorter-run, near-term goals as a starting point. If horizon goals are set first, however, your business will necessarily be analyzed in terms of the distant future. Thus, horizon goals must reflect your company's vision. All subsequent plans aim toward the longer-term goal rather than being unduly constrained with meeting near-term profitability or sales targets. At the very least, horizon goals should be developed for sales dollars, market share, dollar profits, cash flow, and return on investment.

Near-term goals are those portions of the horizon goals that can logically be attained in a short time. For example, if the planning horizon for a manufacturing firm is five years and the horizon goal is to increase sales by 50 percent, then the near-term goal could logically be to increase sales by 10 percent over the next year. Similarly, a restaurant manager may have a three-year planning horizon and may want to have a new restaurant in place at the end of the three years. A near-term goal may be to accrue $100,000 in interest-bearing accessible funds by the middle of the current fiscal year while keeping the current ratio above 2.25. Near-term goals are the in-progress portion of horizon goals.

From a planning perspective, horizon goals should be established before other goals.

151

Once horizon and near-term goals have been determined, the final goal-setting task is to segment the near-term goals into *target* goals. Target goals refer to very short-term goals that are quite specific in time and measurability. Target goals may generate actions that must be completed in a few weeks or even a few days.

Suppose a growing real estate business in Indianapolis has as one of its horizon goals to increase its market share for residential sales by 10 percent within five years. This goal may then be segmented into the near-term goal of increasing market share by 1 percent in year one, 2 percent in each of years two, three, and four, and 3 percent in year five. Target goals are then developed to refine the near-term goals into smaller increments—increasing home sales by 10 percent in the first quarter, increasing listings by 20 percent, increasing sales per broker by 5 percent, and any other goal that will ultimately lead to the first-year 1 percent increase in market share. Finally, specific actions are planned to achieve those target goals.

Once all the target goals are defined, they must then be checked to ensure that they mesh with the larger or longer near-term goals.

The key to target goals is to make them very specific, measurable, and attainable. Once all the target goals are defined, they must then be checked to ensure that they mesh with the larger or longer near-term goals. Some target goals will change monthly, some will change weekly, and very specific targets might change daily. Although target goals should be included in the strategic plan, they should be physically easy to remove (included in an appendix, for example), because the targets may change frequently. But it is still necessary to write down the target goals and their related activities in order to communicate them, get commitment, and help direct your employees.

The Goal Segmentation Process

The process of strategic goal setting is the same for company-level and unit-level goals. In fact, there should be horizon and near-term goals for both company and unit levels (see Figure 13-4). Target goals are generally developed for the units of the company.

Unfortunately, many business people develop goal statements that are so broad and ambiguous that they are merely platitudes. These dream-list approaches do little to provide a clear focus and direction for business activity or to offer meaningful indicators of business progress or necessary corrective actions. Moving incrementally from horizon to target goals will force you to work through this potential goal stalemate and to produce a series of relevant and significant target goals.

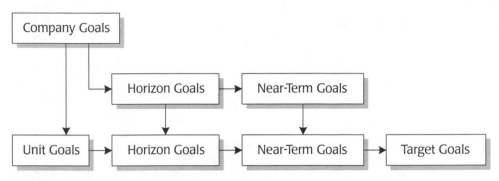

Figure 13-4. Horizon and near-term goals at company and unit levels

Target Action Plans[3]

Once a set of horizon, near-term, and target goals has been developed and communicated, you may sense that planning has been accomplished and that further refinement is unnecessary. However, if you stop here, you probably won't achieve your goals—and you will be frustrated at having spent so much time on the process.

A target action plan, outlined in Figure 13-5, will help you move beyond this bleak possibility. It itemizes a series of tasks to be prescribed and accomplished in meeting each target goal.

The chart shows the target action plan for Uplands Supply, Inc., a growing manufacturer of ink cartridges used in copiers, fax machines, and printers. Uplands decided to use an advertising specialty campaign to promote its sales of ink cartridges to manufacturers of equipment that use the cartridges.

The first step in the target action plan is to restate the target goal in clear, precise, objective, results-oriented terms. In the Uplands example, the target goal is to develop an advertising specialty campaign within the next month, part of a larger near-term goal to increase sales by 15 percent over the next year. Even though the decision to use the advertising specialty approach had already been made, staff commitment to this approach has not been secured. With the target goal firmly in mind, a series of important action steps come into play, including determining any barriers that must be overcome, determining specific tasks that must be done, setting deadlines for completion, and identifying elements of feedback to use to assess results.

Conquering Barriers

Barriers are the obstacles or bottlenecks that must be overcome or circumvented in order to reach target goals. It is critical that you take the time to

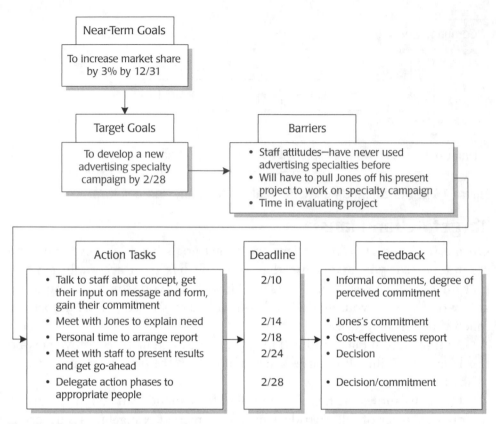

Figure 13-5. A target action plan

consider, in detail, the barriers that stand in your way. Barriers typically relate to human resources, other resources, and time. There are three types of barriers: insurmountable barriers, barriers that can be overcome but only with a concerted redirection of effort toward the barrier, and barriers that can be hurdled en route to the target goals.

The first type is a barrier or a series of barriers so overwhelming and significant that it is clear the target goal will never be attained. Suppose, for example, a company has a target goal of completing a marketing research project by the end of the month. If the two primary researchers on this project suddenly resign, the goal becomes unreachable. It is important to recognize an insurmountable barrier early in the action process before you waste important resources and become frustrated. When you hit an insurmountable barrier, you need to abandon your target goal and consider alternatives.

The second type of barrier must be resolved in order to reach target goals. This kind of barrier prompts you to abandon the target goal temporarily and focus on overcoming the barrier. For example, if a machine is not performing to specifications, the target goal must be set aside and energies directed toward repairing the machine or acquiring a new one. Only then can you pursue the target goal.

The third type of barrier is not as overwhelming but still requires some sacrifice of resources or time. You must be aware of these sacrifices and be open and responsive to addressing these difficulties and explaining the likely benefits of overcoming them. In the Uplands Supply example, the owners must convince the marketing department that time spent on advertising specialties is worthwhile and meaningful. They must also let the staff know what is expected of them, allaying their fears and apprehensions and encouraging a positive, supportive attitude.

Action Tasks

Action tasks are the specific tasks that must be completed to achieve target goals. They are the final step in the process of segmenting goals into smaller, incremental units. These tasks, some of which may focus on dealing with barriers, are very basic and narrowly defined. Each necessary action task must be noted. Once action tasks have been prescribed, they must be arranged into a logical sequence according to their priority.

The specificity of the actions depends on the owner's confidence in employees. If employees are knowledgeable, dedicated, and innovative, action tasks are best stated in broad parameters, leaving it to the employees to determine specific activities. Conversely, if employees are new or unskilled, they may need more specificity and direction.

Deadlines

It is important to establish deadlines, or completion dates, for each task in the sequence. The deadlines must be real, not arbitrary, so employees treat them seriously. Imposing an unnecessarily early deadline only frustrates employees, who no doubt have a number of simultaneous responsibilities. Deadlines should also be meaningful. Those for the most critical tasks—ones that if delayed will cause severe problems—should be set first. Deadlines for other tasks can then be assigned and arranged according to their priority.

It is important to establish deadlines, or completion dates, for each task in the sequence. The deadlines must be real, not arbitrary, so employees treat them seriously.

Feedback

You should have some method of securing feedback in order to evaluate whether a task has been completed or is progressing as required. Feedback

155

should give you a solid feel for the results or status of the task. Feedback regarding individual tasks may be easily identifiable, such as when an employee obtains a contract, or may be more qualitative, such as favorable comments from customers or an apparent increase in the ratio between sales calls and sales dollars. Monitoring feedback allows you to concentrate on action tasks and evaluate efforts to meet each part of the action task sequence. In the Uplands Supply example, action tasks are listed in sequence according to their priority, along with deadlines and a means of evaluative feedback for each.

Bringing It All Together

Thus far, we have identified four elements of strategic planning. First, the firm's mission and vision must be determined. Then, a broad situational analysis is performed, allowing the business to recognize its threats, opportunities, strengths, weaknesses, and relevant competencies. Companywide strategies must be developed, based on opportunities and threats, distinctive competencies, and the overall growth strategy chosen. In the next step, a series of goals is developed in the form of written, measurable goal statements. This series of goals clearly and specifically designates desired results. Finally, a target action plan is enacted to detail the process of achieving the goals. Figure 13-6 outlines this integrative goal model.

Putting It into Practice

As many key people as possible should be brought into the goal-setting process, even though the process can generate conflict among them.

Setting goals is not easy. As many key people as possible should be brought into the goal-setting process, even though the process can generate conflict among them. If one person sees that a new or redefined goal shortchanges a preferred project, conflict can arise.

You should move carefully and cautiously here. A number of iterations may be necessary before goals are finalized. Communication is all-important. We suggest you adopt the mantra, "Communicate, communicate, communicate." In setting goals you need to consider changes in how the company operates to meet those goals. Because growth is occurring or is desired, you must continually encourage your people to adapt to new strategies, new structures, and new goals despite any natural resistance. Thus, the goal-setting process must be handled carefully and with constant attention to the company's vision and mission. We will say more about how you can help

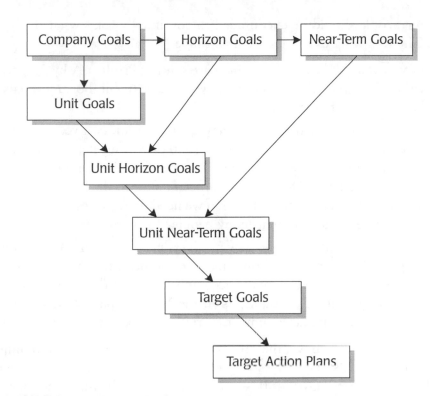

Figure 13-6. Integrative goal model

this process along later in the book when we look at leading change.

We recommend that you keep in mind the characteristics of good goals:

▶ specific

▶ measurable and attainable

▶ challenging yet realistic

▶ tangible and phrased in terms of outcomes rather than processes

By focusing on outcomes, you can avoid getting bogged down in either processes or resource allocation. As part of the communication process, it is necessary to instill in everyone's mind that it is the final result desired that drives everything else. If you can develop an intensive focus on goals and results, then the goals become the unifying force for your company. Once people agree on goals, conflicts over resource allocation, company priorities, and strategies tend to subside. And once the mindset of key employees is clearly focused on goals and results, it is easier to work on refining and segmenting goals in terms of timelines and levels within the organization.

Your people should be encouraged to continually ask "what if?" questions. The following examples are illustrative:

▶ "If you want the company to increase sales of Product A by 20 percent within three years, what should be your departmental or unit goals for the next year? For the next quarter?"

▶ "If we anticipate that our sales may double within two years (based on an analysis of the industry), what resources will we need to make that happen? How many employees will we need to hire? How many managers will we need? Do we have sufficient staff in the human resources department to accomplish that? Do we need to adjust our salary schedules in order to attract that many people?"

▶ "If we want to develop two new products per year in order to maintain the growth we envision, how much do we need to invest in research and development to ensure the accomplishment of the goal? Should we add more scientists or engineers in the R&D department, or can we gain more product development by restructuring into project teams?"

As seen from the above, the process of goal setting is often more important than the goals themselves because it encourages everyone to work together. We feel strongly that this unifying force is well worth the time you spend on it.

Notes

1. Patricia Sellers, "Most Powerful Women in Business," *Fortune*, www.fortune.com (accessed October 9, 2004) and www.ebay.com (accessed October 9, 2004).

2. Lewis Carroll, *Alice's Adventures in Wonderland* (New York: The Place and Peck Company, 1900), pp. 62-63.

3. Many of the ideas for this action plan are drawn from the goal-planning work of the Center for Creative Leadership, Greensboro, North Carolina.

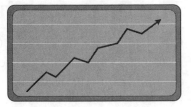

Chapter 14

Championing Change

ANDY TAYLOR FACED A TOUGH CHALLENGE WHEN HE TOOK OVER THE reins of a successful and rapidly growing business, Enterprise Rent-a-Car, in 1980. Unfortunately, the speed of Enterprise's growth actually *was* the problem. Quality was slipping and customer complaints were escalating. The core philosophy of "customers and employees first" seemed to have taken a back seat. Taylor knew that decisive changes had to be made. He instituted the Enterprise Service Quality index to measure customer opinion and tied the index to the company's promotion system. Not surprisingly, customer service took center stage—an outcome that Taylor believes was fundamental to the 350 percent growth Enterprise has experienced over the last 10 years. And it has helped make Enterprise the largest car rental company in North America.[1]

Although Taylor's situation and strategies for building growth may be quite different from yours, you face a common challenge—leading your business through change. This book has concentrated on strategic thinking and the process of strategic planning for growth. But strategic planning is always linked to the challenge of leading change. Many leaders try to ignore this link. And that is why so many well-formulated strategic plans just sit on the shelf and do little to affect a firm's direction. So, before we conclude, we must consider some practical thoughts on taking that next step—leading change.

159

The Drive for Change

Change is a constant of life. Change breathes life into businesses and organizations. Change is one of the features of being an aggressive, growth-oriented, opportunity-driven business in a rapidly shifting, complex marketplace. Part of your task, as the leader of your business, is to help those in your business understand and accept that they must embrace change. That means you must help your people understand that change is part of growth and success. They must also understand that what brought success in yesterday's markets may not be enough today.

Sometimes, a company's entire strategic focus needs to change. When John Thompson took over the helm at Symantec in 1999, the firm was experiencing moderate success. However, the consumer software company lacked a core technology and fielded a portfolio of largely unrelated products. Thompson recognized market vulnerability and the need for strategic planning. He held a strategic retreat for his senior management team and addressed, head on, the question of future growth. Building on the strength of the company's popular Norton AntiVirus program, a clear growth strategy that focused the business on Internet security emerged. Next, the managers made bold change moves. They trimmed unrelated products from Symantec's portfolio. To beef up the company's presence in enterprise security for corporate clients, they made a series of acquisitions. These were huge moves that changed Symantec dramatically. Looking back over the past few years, Thompson sounds an important message. "There is almost nothing about the company today ... that is anywhere near what we had in 1999."[2]

You must be willing to accept the same drive for change. This does not mean that you throw out everything and build from scratch. It does mean that you are always taking a careful and objective look at yourself and your environment. And it means that you are willing to act—and act boldly—when necessary. Successful businesses are always modifying their products and making market adjustments based on trends and emerging opportunities.

Try this quiz: what is the product being described? It is growing in popularity among older consumers. Sales have grown 500 percent in a recent five-year period. Professionals are buying it for their commutes to the office. Getting warm? Try this clue. It is a 70-miles-per-gallon form of transportation that's been around for years. Got it? Scooters are hot sellers. While companies like Vespa and Yamaha have produced scooters for a long time, the vehicle is undergoing a facelift. These companies are producing a new scooter—one that is more powerful and highway-friendly. You see, the market has changed. It's no longer just an older or leisure market. Now, commuters are the draw. And there is promising potential in that market.[3]

You should be building, through your statements and actions, a culture of change. That's a strong statement, but that culture must be present in a growing business. This means that change should be one of the key values that define your organization. That may seem extreme, but it is not. Think of the values, the core values that define your firm—quality, customer service, integrity, and probably a few other closely related items. Change should be one of these items too. It must be part of who you are and what you do.

Change is a core cultural value of growth-oriented businesses. Rather than being an unwanted intruder, change is part of the family.

It Doesn't Come Easy

Although we realize that change is a reality of business life, there is another reality that also must be considered. Change can be one of the most divisive and crippling issues a business encounters.

At the strategic level, most of us understand why change is needed. Without change, there is no progress. In fact, without change, you can't even keep up. In your business, marked by constant competition, a reluctance to change is a sure fire formula for long-run disaster.

However, change does not take place at the strategic level. It is, instead, an extremely personal move. Change threatens what we understand. It shakes us from our comfort zone. And that is where the rub comes. At the personal level, many of us would rather not mess with the wrenching complexity of change. Even when the status quo is not all we desire, it is often safer and easier to grumble than get busy with the struggle and stress of changing. Make no mistake: that is exactly where a number of people in your business are sitting right now!

There is nothing strange about such resistance to change. For many people, caught in the rapid pace of their daily lives, holding change at arm's length is a reasonable way to cope and a logical way to survive. Is turf protection involved? Sure! Is there a desire to maintain and preserve one's current status and sense of value in the organizational system? Absolutely! Is there an honest belief that one more thing cannot be placed on an already overflowing plate? You bet! Importantly, each of these responses is honest and understandable.

Given this backdrop, how does change, particularly important business change, ever get enacted? While difficult and involved, change happens through people. And a decision to pay too little attention to people will, most likely, doom your efforts of change. As we will describe, change rests on a foundation of four pillars. Further, it is our conviction that most significant change efforts that fail do so because one of these foundation pillars has been ignored.

The Four Pillars of Change

Leading successful change rests on four pillars. These pillars become foundations or grounding stakes for your change efforts. The four pillars we present here are neither novel nor earth-shattering. Yet these pillars, when carefully considered and addressed, bridge the chasm of change—a chasm that comes from the natural resistance and general confusion that typically accompany change. Let's explore each of these pillars.

Pillar One: Selling the Change

The first thing your people need during change is a sense of logic. When people recognize and appreciate the underlying logic of change, they tend to approach change differently. Consider what happens when people are not provided this base of logic. They draw extreme assumptions. They magnify even minor issues. Negative spins begin to emerge and become predominant. Importantly, without logic, most people fail to place credibility in managers or their capacity to lead change. And, when credibility is shaken, the chances of successfully delivering change are greatly reduced.

Therefore, leading change begins with selling the change or, more precisely, selling the need for change. Harvard professor John Kotter, an expert on organizational change, believes that selling the change is the most critical step in the entire change process. Kotter even states the case more strongly, noting that leaders have to create a "sense of urgency."[5] When you create a sense of urgency, you are convincing your people that there is absolutely no option other than change. Staying with the status quo is simply not a reasonable path to continue. You are convincing your people that the business simply cannot accept and live with the outcomes of not changing. Interestingly, this approach is drawn from the principle that most of us get serious about change only when the pain of staying where we are is greater than the pain incurred in changing.

The responsibility for selling the change falls on you and your leadership team. Further, you must translate your understanding of the need for change in such clear and obvious terms that others recognize, comprehend, and

Columbia University professor and author Michael Feiner says it succinctly. "Leading change is one of the cardinal objectives of a leader."[4]

accept the conclusion that change must occur. While you will never convince everyone, you must convince most folks.

Often, leaders dread and shy from the time-consuming processes of building the case for change and selling the change. This is unfortunate. Make no mistake: most change efforts fail here.

This step requires heavy doses of communication. It requires sharing some key evidence. It requires effort on your part. Yet, when you have sold your people on the need for change, your business focus shifts from holding firmly to what has always been done to looking for new ways to make the business better.

Ideally, you should sell the problem before you even begin formal strategic planning. In that way, your people can see the planning process as it unfolds. They will not know all the details. But they will know that something is going on and they will know that a team is working to address the problems at hand. This tends to legitimize planning for people throughout the business. And your strategic planning activities take on a whole new role and purpose.

There are times when selling the need for change is not all that difficult. Consider this example. Despite a 22-year record of success, Mike Sheldrake's business, Polly's Gourmet Coffee, was rocked by a powerful new competitor—Starbucks. Suddenly, growth was not the issue. Survival was. Through a careful focus strategy, Sheldrake targeted the high-end, upscale customer and created a more specialized, unique niche for Polly's.[6] It probably wasn't hard to sell the change given the probable disaster Polly's faced if it didn't change.

Selling the change becomes more difficult when your business is successful and you are pursuing new opportunities for growth. People need to understand the opportunity and why it must be seized now. Further, they must realize the downside of not acting. Remember that most people get comfortable and rather set in their ways. Your job, as a leader of your business, is to guide the search for new opportunities and win over others by explaining why these opportunities make sense.

Selling the change becomes more difficult when your business is successful and you are pursuing new opportunities for growth.

Consider the story of Amar Bose, the audio-equipment pioneer whose Bose speakers are No. 1 in the home speaker market. How does Bose plan to grow? You may be surprised. While it will continue to reinvest in R&D to improve technology and create innovative sound products, Bose's latest product is a new car suspension system. Even for a technology-rich company like Bose, this is a dramatic change. Will its new technology revolutionize the auto industry? Part of Amar Bose and his leadership team's job is to sell the logic of this change.[7]

We can anticipate at least two concerns you have right now.

First, you may be reluctant to share too much about the business and how it is doing. If you are the owner or the guiding entrepreneur of the business, the tendency to "hold close to the numbers" is understandable. There is always information that cannot and should not be shared. However, we encourage you to share enough to build and sell the case for change. It will pay dividends in fighting off resistance and having your people support change.

Second, you are probably concerned about time. You are busy. You're already running at full speed and the last thing you want to do is spend time selling the change. We can only tell you that it is time and effort well spent. Further, taking the time up front staves off all sorts of problems as the change unfolds.

Pillar Two: Selling the Strategy

Selling the change does not prescribe what we will do. Rather, it builds the case for why change is needed. The second pillar of change is offering people a strategy for change. It is the leader's responsibility to frame the strategy of change. We assume that this strategy has emerged from your strategic planning process. It becomes your responsibility to sell the strategy too.

At this point, you simply want to sell your people on the broad, general strategy that you will be pursuing. You are providing them with a sense of direction and why that direction makes sense. This should follow logically from the case for change that you have already built. You want to present a picture of the planned strategy. You want to present it simply enough so that everybody can understand its meaning and implications. Yet, the strategy, hopefully, will be so captivating that it becomes a rallying point for the efforts of change. It's important that the strategy be so clear, so motivational, so essential, and so fundamental that a "commitment to the new approach" emerges among your people.

We are not going to mince words here. This really is a selling job. Too many leaders believe that once they and their strategic planning team have concluded their planning process, all that remains is to give a waiting organization its marching orders. This is a dangerous approach. Your people will probably be cautious. The time you spend selling the strategy will help them feel included. It will build energy and support for the success of the strategy. And it will minimize the level of resistance that you encounter.

Don't expect totally smooth sailing at this point. Expect concerns, questions, and even criticisms. Our advice: listen, answer, and evaluate. Listen to their concerns. Answer their questions. Evaluate their criticisms. Listening to

> "Faced with the choice between changing one's mind and proving that there is no need to do so, almost everybody gets busy on the proof."
> –John Kenneth Galbraith

concerns will help you understand your people and what fears are being stoked by the changes you are going to pursue. Answering your people openly and candidly will enhance trust and minimize rumors. Finally, don't be afraid to objectively evaluate the criticisms you hear. Your people just might be on to something. They may uncover a flaw or needed action that you and the planning team did not consider. Use their input and criticism as an opportunity to fine-tune your plans. Resist the "not invented here" fallacy. Just because you and your core team of strategic thinkers didn't come up with an idea or foresee a possible glitch does not mean that it does not make sense or is any less real.

At this point, most people realize that all the details of change have not been worked out. But if you can build a sense of excitement for where you are headed, your people can actually help you fill in the details. Getting their ideas and letting them have a chance to offer input helps people feel like they have some ownership in the change. Accordingly, they are much more likely to support and work for the change to be a success.

Pillar Three: Providing Connection

The third pillar of change is connection. One of the key things that people need during change is connection. Change is a personal experience. People want and need to know how the change will affect them at the deepest, most personal level. Their questions are basic and legitimate. Where do I fit in? What part will I play? Exactly what will my role be? In short, people need to know how they connect to the change.

The need for connection is a powerful individual need. It provides people with a sense of significance—the feeling that they are important, that they count, that they make a difference, and that they are needed. Part of the popularity of teams in organizations today comes from the increased sense of connection and significance that often accompanies team activity.

Unfortunately, connection threatens to unravel during change. Some may believe, and at times rightly so, that existing working relationships will be destroyed or displaced by the changes you are outlining and pursuing. Some fear that their status among their peers will be affected. Others wonder whether friendships that have formed on the job will be threatened by changed patterns of contact.

Again, communication becomes a key. Talk with your people. Listen to their concerns. Listen to their resistance. Let's look at this theme of resistance just a bit further.

Turn the communication faucet wide open as your people work through change. Unfortunately, many leaders turn the faucet off or provide, at best, a slow drip during change. It is nearly impossible to overcommunicate during change.

There is nothing strange about resistance to change. Those who resist are neither weaker performers nor more fragile personalities. Rather—and here is a bold notion—resistance is a normal, psychologically healthy response that people have to all that is happening and changing. Any leader can force people to quiet their resistance, at least in his or her presence. Leaders can force people to suppress their resistance. But that does not make the feelings of resistance go away.

Creative leaders allow their people to express resistance. These leaders listen to, consider, and respond to the pockets of resistance that their people present. At times, this resistance may appear to be little more than carping or complaining. A little of that is OK and can even be beneficial, as long as people realize that we are not retreating. We can't. Remember: we have already sold the problem, and we have sold the strategy. Jeanie Duck has a great phrase for this. She says to tell your people, "You can visit Pity City, but you aren't allowed to move there."[8]

Listening to resistance provides you with some very good input. It helps you know what is going on rather than just assume.

Listening to resistance provides you with some very good input. It helps you know what is going on rather than just assume. It also enhances your credibility and engenders more trust during the change.

You may not feel comfortable with this move, but think about the alternative—not listening. The resistance will still be there. People will still talk among themselves. Rumors will likely run rampant. And now, it's all behind the scenes, outside your realm of direct awareness. Hopefully, you'd rather know what's going than hear it thirdhand after a major part of the change effort has failed.

After listening, respond as honestly and fully as you can to the questions and concerns that people pose. There will be questions you cannot answer. Say so.

We recently worked with midsized business whose leadership team decided on a new direction. This would require a substantial change in the company's core business too. Understandably, people were concerned. Restructuring was necessary. The leader held a series of open meetings and addressed concerns (resistance) as best he could. He was able to squelch some rumors. And he heard a couple of issues—particularly concerns about possible outsourcing—that simply were untrue. He now was able to clarify and reassure and resolve what could have erupted into big motivational problems.

Help your people see where and how they fit into the new business plans. As stated earlier, you may even want to give your people a chance to be involved in the change. For some, this involvement will come as they help define and outline the needed changes through the strategic planning process. For others, having a role in implementing the change will work. But involvement will help them feel a greater sense of connection.

Pillar Four: Reinforcing the Change

The fourth pillar of change is reinforcing the change. You sold your people on the need for change and you sold them on the direction. In a way, you sold them that things would be better for the business because of the changes being made. Now you have to convince them that the change really does make sense, that things really are better. You need to do this carefully and regularly and often. And you need to do it this in a variety of ways.

Listen to resistance. It's a signal that your people have real concerns that need attention.

First, celebrate the successes you have. In the early phases of change, celebrate often. The celebration does not have to be elaborate. It can simply be recognizing an accomplishment associated with the change and making sure that people know about it. Look for opportunities to reinforce and celebrate. If you land a new client, let people know. Thank them. Tie the new client to the change. In other words, let people know that this new client is evidence that things are working and that your change is on the right track.

Talk about the change a lot. Mention the change and the successes it is bringing. Do this through various forms of communication. If you have a company newsletter, be sure you include items on the change. When you give speeches or talk to people, you should look for opportunities to let people know about the progress of change. Remember that you want to keep the change effort foremost in people's minds and you want to create positive buzz for the change.

Look at your reward system. Is it consistent with the new change goals? This is important. As we all know, people do what they are rewarded for doing. People embrace change when they realize that doing so affects their bottom line. Don't ignore this key point.

In all these ways, some formal and some far more casual, you are convincing people to "live the change." And you are convincing them to work hard for the change.

What Now?

Growth and change go hand in hand. In order to grow, a drive for change must be present in your business. The themes and pillars we have presented become keys to for successful change. Importantly, paying attention to these ideas will help your people be more open to the next change .... It's probably just around the corner.

Notes

1. Kemp Powers, "How We Got Started: Andy Taylor," *Fortune Small Business*, September 2004, p. 104.

2. Ellen Florian, "Six Lessons from the Fast Lane," *Fortune*, September 6, 2004, pp. 146-156.

3. Daniel Nassau, "Scooters Catch On with Commuters, Despite Safety Issues," *The Wall Street Journal*, September 30, 2004, p. D4.

4. Michael Feiner, *The Feiner Points of Leadership* (New York: Warner Business Books, 2004), p. 193.

5. John P. Kotter, *Leading Change* (Boston: Harvard Business School Press, 1996).

6. Joshua Hyatt, "Beat the Beast," *Fortune Small Business*, September 2004, pp. 42-48.

7. Brian Dumaine, "How We Got Started: Amar Bose," *Fortune Small Business,* September 2004, pp. 92-95.

8. Jeanie Daniel Duck, "Managing Change: The Art of Balancing," in *Harvard Business Review On Change* (Boston: Harvard Business School Publishing, 1998), p. 68.

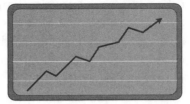

Chapter 15

Get It
in Writing

B Y THIS TIME, YOU SHOULD HAVE A GOOD FEEL FOR WHAT GOES INTO a strategic plan. You realize the need for both an external analysis of your company's environment and an objective analysis of your resources and capabilities. You understand the nature of distinctive competencies, growth strategies, and goals. But one more task remains: to put the analysis into a written document that can be read by the people with a vested interest in how the firm competes. With this in mind, when you finish this chapter, you should be able to write a plan that fulfills the purposes discussed throughout the book.

This chapter reviews the items to include in the strategic plan and discusses the format and writing. Recall in Chapter 2 that we divided the strategic planning process into three phases: providing the vision and mission of the business, the analysis, and the actions necessary to develop the strategy. The final step of the action phase is the actual writing of the plan.

Why Write the Plan?

Many business managers make the dangerous assumption that a plan can be stored in their minds and still give them needed direction and guidance. Although the strategic plan is primarily an instrument for guiding leaders, others also read it too. Employees, for example, can benefit from being aware of where the business is headed. For many businesses, investors are also keenly interested in reading the plan. At times, suppliers or even potential customers may want to read it. Even though some items in the written plan may seem trite or self-evident to you, they may be necessary for others. You may need to share the plan or portions of the plan with investors, lenders, key suppliers, or perhaps even other businesses that might be partners in a strategic alliance.

Even though some items in the written plan may seem trite or self-evident to you, they may be necessary for others.

Reasonably specific detail should be included—as much detail as confidentiality allows. These details are necessary. Remember that a second key use of the plan is to review progress. The more specific the plan, the better progress can be evaluated. Less obvious is the motivational effect of putting the plan on paper.

The Strategic Plan Format

Figure 15-1 shows the format for a strategic plan. This is followed by a detailed discussion of the format.

I. Create a winning mission statement
  A. Product line or services provided
  B. Company vision
  C. Company philosophy and values
II. Identify growth opportunities
  A. Broad-based environmental characteristics
  B. Industry-specific environmental characteristics
III. Determine distinctive competencies
IV. Generate growth strategies and goals
  A. Growth strategies
  B. Company goals
V. Plan actions

Figure 15-1. The plan for writing the plan

Create a Mission Statement

The written mission statement (see Chapter 4) needs be no more than one or two paragraphs, although some may be a bit longer. The mission statement must lay out the general direction of your company and describe the firm's product line or groups of product lines. It should also briefly discuss your business philosophy and vision. And it should be specific enough to let the reader assess how the business operates and how its culture, tone, or climate appears to the public.

Identify Growth Opportunities

This section of the plan is a broad overview of your business, intended to give potential readers a feel for the business and its operating environment. It need not be excessively detailed, but it should provide the reader with a solid understanding of your firm and the key dynamics affecting its operation.

Initially, it should discuss opportunities in the broad-based environment because general environmental factors affect all businesses. Even so, note whether the company is a wholesale, manufacturing, retail, or service business.

Next, provide a fairly detailed discussion of the industry in which you compete. You should include the industry's sensitivity to the economy, the intensity of competition, the nature of competition (price vs. quality vs. product differentiation), and the size of the total market. Specific information on competitors should follow. Estimate each competitor's market share and other significant competitive factors. Include any additional relevant information about key competitors. Taken together, the industry and competitors' data should provide a reasonably clear idea of the size of the market and the degree of turbulence to expect. The data should also give the reader an idea of where the business fits within the industry.

Determine Distinctive Competencies

Explain your distinctive competencies, with the degree of detail dependent on the intended audience. If the primary readers are inside the organization, you should include a fairly specific rendering of distinctive competencies to help employees understand your perception of the firm's key strengths, which may also be useful if lenders or other investors will be reading the plan. On the other hand, if suppliers, customers, or others outside the firm have access to the plan, then you should give a more conservative, less detailed presentation of the distinctive competencies so as not to tip off competitors about proprietary information.

Explain your distinctive competencies, with the degree of detail dependent on the intended audience.

Generate Growth Strategies and Goals

This section lays out in more detail the direction in which your business is headed. It also focuses on more specific goals, both for the business as a whole and for the units within the business.

Growth Strategies. The strategies that you will pursue in order to grow should be explained well, including their justification. Remember that a growth strategy is an overall, general plan or approach for running the firm in response to its external and internal conditions. (Refer to Chapter 12.) The description of the individual strategies in the plan must be detailed enough to make their precise nature clear.

Company Goals. While the mission statement lets readers know where the business is headed and growth strategies prescribe a general business approach for getting there, company goals enable the reader to see the specific achievements or results you expect the business to reach. Include company goals covering both the horizon and the near term. Present the two time frames so that readers can clearly see the relationship between the near-term goals and the broader horizon goals.

As noted in Chapter 13, horizon goals are oriented toward the overall planning horizon, so these goals are stated in broad terms. Near-term goals concentrate on the next business operating period and require greater precision, detail, and specificity. Horizon and near-term goals are fundamental, critical elements in the written plan. Goal statements are one of the primary factors that outside readers focus on in assessing the business, its scope of activities, and the plausibility of its intended direction. In addition, near-term goals become the key benchmarks for monitoring and evaluating business operations. Their effects on internal direction and control, as well as on external perceptions of the business, are quite significant.

Plan Actions

Oftentimes, when managers write a strategic plan, it becomes nothing more than a tiresome exercise in persistence. You may complete an in-depth analysis of your markets, provide an objective assessment of your own company, and identify some legitimate strategies. You may think that it's finally done and you may even be energized about your plan when you leave the last planning session. Unfortunately, when you return to your office, the inbox is piled high. Putting out day-to-day fires takes precedence and the strategic plan gets pushed to the back burner. Enough about planning—time to get back to reality, right? Wrong!

Why is it that so many strategic plans end up sitting on the shelf collecting dust? The reason—no discernable action plan. You may come up with the greatest strategies in the world, but if you don't develop a plan of attack to implement these strategies, what good are they? Action planning is truly where the rubber meets the road. It is the process of taking your growth strategies and company goals and breaking them down into doable tasks. Action planning should identify:

► the individual accountable for each goal

► specific timelines and milestones for each goal

► resources needed to achieve each goal

► metrics for success

Action planning is a critical last step to writing your plan. By taking goals down to ground level, your plan can make a difference.

Sharing the Plan

Once you have written the strategic plan, what should you do with it? Of course, you must communicate it to key people in the firm (although many of them were no doubt involved in developing the plan). Debate arises over how widely to distribute the plan.

Some argue that sharing the plan provides employees with a keener sense of where the business is headed and thereby improves their dedication and motivation. The same logic could apply to key suppliers or those with whom the business is building strategic links or alliances. If the workforce is small and viewed as stable and loyal, it's a good idea to share at least part of the plan, if not all of it, with everyone. Similarly, if alliances are strong and enduring, sharing the plan or key portions of it makes sense.

If the workforce is small and viewed as stable and loyal, it's a good idea to share at least part of the plan, if not all of it, with everyone.

The other side of the debate deals with the real need for security and the protection of sensitive information. For example, there is some risk that an employee may take the information from the plan and either join a competitor or start a competing business. Also, other businesses may use information from the plan to their competitive advantage. In these cases, excerpts from the plan may be the preferred route. Employees, for example, could be given the goal section of the plan, and more sensitive items could be shared only with top management. You may need to show the complete plan or portions of it to investors, suppliers, or key customers, but it's a good idea not to show sensitive information to outside groups unless it's specifically required.

Putting It into Action

You should encourage managers to differentiate between an annual business plan—used in the budgeting process or in pursuing financing—and the strategic plan—used to guide the company's long-term performance. The strategic plan has a different flavor or tone from the business plan, which is written with short-term horizons in mind. The purpose of the business plan is to effectively allocate resources for the coming year or to generate interest in providing capital to the firm. The strategic plan, on the other hand, is written objectively and is for the benefit of people inside the firm; it shouldn't be glossy or unduly optimistic. The object is not to impress but to provide guidance and benchmarks for the future.

Some managers may resist a lot of detail, but the trend is to provide more information to those within the firm.

A second issue for consideration is the level of detail in the strategic plan. Generally, more detail is better. Some managers may resist a lot of detail, but the trend is to provide more information to those within the firm. This is especially true in growth-oriented businesses, as most of the employees may be committing many, many hours to the company. Therefore, a detailed plan may increase their motivation to understand where the company is headed and what its current status is.

Finally, you will need to communicate the plan to all interested people and to set a specific time for a review of the company's progress. A review should be done at least three to six months after the plan is written but no later than a year after. At least one quarter is necessary for changes in the firm's strategy or environment to be noticeable. Thus, progress should be ascertained at the end of the quarter after the plan is written or at the end of the succeeding quarter. This is not to say that monthly performance should be ignored, but from a strategic viewpoint, a somewhat longer time frame may be more useful. On the other hand, waiting longer than a year to review the company's progress negates the usefulness of the plan. Any time longer than that may reveal so many changes in the firm's internal status, its strategy, or its economic and competitive environment that no one could determine any cause-and-effect relationship.

It is crucial to write very specific items into the final strategic planning document, a document so detailed and clearly written that all interested parties can understand where the firm is headed and how it plans to get there. In addition, the written document serves as a control measure and an evaluative device at the end of the quarter, fiscal year, or other key time period.

A Final Caveat

We've attempted throughout this book to provide as much information as possible to aid in the creation of a strategic plan for growth-oriented businesses. You may still be reluctant to take the time necessary to analyze the environment, assess the strengths and weaknesses of the business, and develop a strategic plan based on the distinctive competencies of the business. The effort, however, should be highly rewarding, not only because of the strategies you actually develop, but because you have taken the time to analyze the firm and its environment objectively. This objective analysis alone is worth the time and effort! A written plan provides additional benefits: it encourages commitment to a specific plan and it offers a mechanism for reviewing progress later. The plan becomes both a measure of success and a method of achieving success. The development and writing of a strategic plan can't guarantee success, but it is a giant stride in the right direction.

Index